THE WHOLE WORLD KIN

THE WHOLE WORLD KIN
DARWIN AND THE SPIRIT OF LIBERAL RELIGION

Fredric Muir, Editor

SKINNER HOUSE BOOKS

BOSTON

Printed in the United States

Cover design by Kathryn Sky-Peck
Text design by Suzanne Morgan
Cover art *Aquarium* by Margret Hofheinz-Döring, © Margret Hofheinz-Döring/ Galerie Brigitte Mauch Göppingen

ISBN 1-55896-556-4
978-1-55896-556-0

12 11 10 09
6 5 4 3 2 1

Library of Congress Cataloging-in-Publication Data

The whole world kin : Darwin and the spirit of liberal religion / Fredric Muir, editor.
    p. cm.
  ISBN-13: 978-1-55896-556-0 (alk. paper)
  ISBN-10: 1-55896-556-4 (alk. paper)
  1. Liberalism (Religion)—Unitarian Universalist Association. 2. Unitarian Universalist Association—Doctrines. 3. Liberalism (Religion)—Unitarian Universalist churches. 4. Life—Religious aspects. 5. Darwin, Charles, 1809-1882. I. Muir, Fredric John.
  BX9841.3.E53 2009
  230'.91–dc22
              2009021177

"At the Smithville Methodist Church," copyright © 1986 by Stephen Dunn, from *New and Selected Poems 1974-1994* by Stephen Dunn, used by permission of W.W. Norton & Company, Inc.

The essay by Minot Judson Savage originally appeared as "The Theory of the World" in *The Religion of Evolution*, published by George H. Ellis in 1876.

Contents

One touch of nature makes the whole world kin.

—William Shakespeare

Foreword

Several years ago, while vacationing on an island off the Maine coast, I found myself sitting on the massive boulders of the rocky cliffs, staring out over the Atlantic Ocean. After a time, I allowed myself to become fully absorbed in the moment and became aware that I was perched not simply on a large rock, but on the edge of evolution. The rocks and their lichens, the graceful cormorants and raucous seagulls, the undulating ocean—we were all there together, products of the creative evolutionary forces that had brought us to this place, bearing witness to the most recent moment in time.

Unitarian Universalists and other religious liberals have always affirmed the fundamental unity and interdependence of all existence, the truth that our world is continuously recreated in a dynamic and open-ended process. The essays collected in *The Whole World Kin* celebrate this reality from a range of perspectives. They offer not simply a defense of evolution—evolution can take care of itself—but an exploration of the many ways that science and religion can be mutually supportive. This is not news to Unitarian Universalists. In 1885, Unitarian theologian Francis Ellingwood Abbot published his book *Scientific Theism*, recasting several traditional theological doctrines in terms of evolution. That same year, Universalist biblical scholar Orello Cone published an essay on "Evolution and Revelation" in the *Universalist Quarterly*, arguing that science, by revealing the grandeur of the universe, was fully supportive of religion. Countless works have appeared since that time, and *The Whole World Kin* continues this heritage.

This book is timely for a number of reasons, not simply because 2009 marks the 200th anniversary of Darwin's birth and the 150th anniversary of the publication of *On the Origin of Species*. Evolution is not only about biology and geology, it is also about culture. Since the famous Scopes trial in 1925, battles over the relationship of religion and science have become a part of our cultural landscape. But culture, too, is open-ended, continually reshaped by evolutionary forces of its own. Both science and religion contribute to this process, just as the culture influences the way science and religion are developed and understood. This is also part of our dynamic interdependence.

Unitarian Universalists and other religious liberals have always understood the critical role that human beings play in this process. Human agency is a product of biological evolution, but the ways we exercise it—the choices we make or fail to make, the relationships we nourish or fail to nourish—contribute to our cultural evolution. This means that our radical interdependence has a moral dimension. Our culture sometimes seems stuck in a permanent battle in which we are asked to choose between faith and knowledge. Yet we religious liberals know that the primary lesson of evolution is that nothing is permanent, and that the reality of interdependence belies the false dualism on which this culture war is based. We have work to do, and the essays in this volume will help.

Some of the most interesting developments in theology in recent decades have involved the integration of science and religion. Many theologians today treat the natural sciences, including physics and biology, not as hindrances, but as fertile theological resources. The authors in this volume offer their own insights to this process of integration from the perspective of religious liberalism. They remind us that we who think of ourselves as religious people need not be afraid of science, nor scientists of religion.

Paul Rasor

Preface

There is grandeur in this view of life, with its several powers, having been originally breathed into a few forms or
into one; and that whilst this planet has gone cycling on
according to the fixed laws of gravity, from so simple a
beginning endless forms most beautiful and most wonderful have been, and are being, evolved.

—*On the Origin of Species*

At the end of the pier that skimmed the lake's surface, I sat and
stared at the still dark green water. The warm, late summer sun felt
good on my small, growing body. I laid back and looked straight
up into the sky where several gulls circled, looking for a meal. I
made the cloud tufts into whatever designs I wanted, I listened to
a passing boat and lapping water on the shoreline, and uninter-
rupted, I sat and imagined.

Rolling over and looking between the horizontal spaces
between the pier's planks, I could see through the uneven shadows
to the sandy bottom dotted with lake grass. Adjusting my percep-
tion so that I wasn't just looking at the bottom or just the reflection
of an eight-year-old's eyes in between the boards—there, floating
between the grasses, effortlessly suspended, with only the slow
but steady rhythmic movement of their pectoral fins, were several fishes. And then, widening my view, I could see more, at least
a dozen. They were all doing the same thing—with no apparent
direction, they were just floating. Were they waiting for something?

Were they observing me? Were they hiding from a predator or the strong sun? I concluded they were resting, taking a break: They were sleeping. As I lay on the cottage pier, watching the motionless, drifting fish, I slipped into a boyhood sleep, cushioned by the warm vacation day and images of water and suspended fish—the stuff of my young life at that moment. Buoyed by the innocence of my age in a stagnant decade, I was sleeping with the fishes.

Though asleep, I was very alive. The floating fish represented neither death nor separation nor Other. Just the opposite—I felt comforted by and connected to something fundamental and basic, something that went to the core and essence of my eight-year-old life. These were not merely fish; they were the very stuff of life, part of an existence we shared equally.

Across cultures and for millennia, fish have symbolized eternity, creativity, happiness, knowledge, fertility. They are metaphors for the transforming spirit, the pulsating life force, giving meaning to everything we know and love. In sleeping with the fishes I had a momentary experience of at-one-ment, an affirmation of our connectedness, an opportunity to imagine living in an interdependent web.

Perhaps because of small excursions of this sort into the natural world, I chose to follow a path that led me to the ministry. The blessings and grounding from that nap on the pier—and countless similar experiences—remain present to me. Charles Darwin followed a different path, but I like to think we had similar motivations. Darwin nearly became an Anglican priest, but in 1831 turned from that journey in order to follow his bliss, natural history. Buoyed by a family of freethinkers, who were both wealthy and socially connected, Darwin never lost the sense of meaning and passion he felt when immersed in the history of nature.

While Darwin's commitment to the church, and then to religion, grew more distant as he aged, it was not true that he ignored religion and the church, or that he received only support or challenge from clergy. His wife, Emma Wedgwood Darwin, was a devout high-church Christian Unitarian and the tension between them was thick. While ignoring their conflicting faiths—hers in God and his in science—was impossible, Charles chose to limit, if not avoid, religious conversations with her. She needed no reminders to worry that they would not spend the hereafter together due to his lack of faith. Charles was well aware of Emma's feelings, as was he of his grandfather's pronouncement that Unitarianism was merely "a feather-bed to catch a falling Christian."

These tensions were small compared to what followed the 1859 publication of *On the Origin of Species*. Responses from the Church of England, and later from the church universal, were just what he dreaded. Scientific and religious orthodoxies were not ready to broaden their views regarding the evolution of species by natural selection no matter what the substantiating data and narrative suggested. While Darwin found very few sympathetic and supportive public voices at first, they grew substantially over time. And what he couldn't find in England, he later found in the United States, where many greeted his message enthusiastically— especially religious liberals, whose reformation of American Protestantism was still in progress.

Darwin's message shook a sleeping, self-satisfied Western culture. Few wanted to hear or were ready for what he shared. For most scholars and clergy, his story simply didn't fit anywhere. His decades of travel, research, and thoughtful reflection set in motion a reimagining and rewriting of a story that human beings had told for millennia, the story about the origins of life. Lest anyone think that Darwin's challenges have become irrelevant over time, one need only tune into today's media, hear the messages from many church pulpits, learn about the challenges to some public school biology classes, and watch the confrontations between science and politics as policy and funding are debated. The implications of Darwin's work are as alive today as they were in Victorian England, and maybe even more so in the United States.

On that sunny August afternoon of my childhood, when I slept with the fishes, Darwin and the spirit of liberal religion were present to me, however rudimentary and immature my framing

of them. That connection has stood the test of time and my ministry. I no more could have verbalized this than Darwin might have
articulated his thoughts when he was eight and attending the Unitarian Church in Shrewsbury. Eventually, it was through an American event that I came to Darwin's ideas. I read about the 1925 trial
of John Scopes in Dayton, Tennessee, in which not just Scopes but
Darwin, evolution, and liberal religion were all on trial. Next came a
short biography, then another, followed by *On the Origin of Species*,
and then more. Now the second Sunday in February is my congregation's annual Darwin Day observance. For me, the spirit of liberal
religion is enhanced and deepened by Darwin's life and thought.

The contributors to this volume name the spirit of liberal religion that is both a part and a result of Darwin's life and work.
"There is grandeur in this view of life," he concluded in the last
paragraph of *Origin*. May this book contribute to that grandeur.

Fredric Muir
October 2009

The Whole World Is God's Temple

Minot Judson Savage

At the National Unitarian Conference in Saratoga (1872), one of
our most widely known ministers was making a speech on our mis-
sionary work; and, in the course of his remarks, he took occasion
to speak slightingly of those who were wasting their time on such
unpractical questions as the antiquity of the world and the origin
of things. He thought there were enough problems of real, pressing,
living importance right about us to absorb all our attention, and
consume all our energy. And a year ago (1875), in Music Hall, in the
course of a lecture on "Our Scandalous Politics," Mr. Parton took
occasion to ridicule those who were troubling their brains over the
theories of Darwin and Spencer, instead of grappling vigorously
with the political evils and social reforms of the day.

Thoughts and utterances like these are natural enough to one
who does not look beneath the superficial movements of the time
for the hidden, and oftentimes remote, spring and causes of the
conditions of things. If one knew nothing of the interior mechanism of a watch, he might think he could make it keep good time
by turning the hands round on the face; but a wiser person would
take it to a watch-maker, and have the origin of the outer movements looked after.

Men who pride themselves on their reputation as "practical"
workers are often very impatient of theories and theorizers. Theo-
rist to them means visionary. They regard him as dwelling in a

cloud-land, and dealing with unsubstantial fancies. They think his fitting representative is the fabled dog on the foot-bridge, who dropped his bone while clutching at a finer looking shadow. They propose to hold by the bone. And yet, if you'll think of it, every man living has his theory of every thing he does; and all his practice is the result of his theory. The farmer who sneers at his neighbor for adopting the "newfangled notions"—the knowledge of chemicals and soils that modern science has revealed to him—and who pins him to the walls of his kitchen with the stigma "theorizer!" is himself a theorizer just the same; only he keeps working away on a theory that consists in bungling tools and guessing experiments and back-breaking hand-labor—a theory that kept his grandfather poor, a theory long since exploded as deficient and half-way—instead of accepting that theory that new investigation and successful practice have proved true. Should a boy at school attempt a problem in mathematics, and pay no attention to the theory, the underlying principles according to which the question could be solved, you would say he ought to exchange his seat for the dunce's block. Watt and Stephenson succeeded in laying the foundations of our present railway system when they discovered the true theory of the laws and application of steam. Von Moltke is the greatest of modern generals because he has the brain to conceive and carry out the most nearly perfect theory of the laws of war. All of us are theorizers who have brains enough to think out, and work along, the lines of any efficient plan in our business. The banker, the merchant, the lawyer, the physician, the minister, each has his theory; and he is successful just according to his ability to discover the true theory of his position, and to carry it out in effective practice. So you might as well talk of practically growing an oak without an acorn as to think of successful practical work divorced from theory.

And now, for a moment, glance at the absurdity of the position assumed by the preacher and lecturer just referred to. Society and state are sick with various maladies which they desire to heal: so, without stopping to waste time and strength on the unpractical questions of the remote origins and causes of the disease, they propose to blister and bleed and cauterize, without any loss of time. An intelligent physician, when called to a patient, does not consider it any waste of time to stop and investigate, and study the symptoms, in order to find out what the matter is; and, the more serious and urgent the disease, the more careful he is to do this.

Now, there is not a single personal, social, political, or religious question of the day that does not run back and root itself in the remotest antiquity of the race. They all grow out of the original nature of humanity, just as the topmost twig or leaf of a two-thousand-year-old tree is the outgrowth of the first germinal principle from which the ancient trunk has sprung. Here is the trouble with most of the "reforms" of the age. They are the outcome of transcendental notions, purely empirical study, or the hasty guesses of enthusiastic persons, who propose to finish in a year a structure the foundations of which God has been centuries in laying. Any true reform must know the drift of the ages, and work in the line of the eternal movements of the universe.

We are now prepared to raise the question as to whether a study of the "theory of the world" is a practical matter. And, in the first place, glance at the facts. All nations on the face of the earth who have been civilized enough to have any thought-out and organized religion have always connected their popular religion with a cosmogony, or theory of the origin of the universe. The character of their gods, their conception of humanity, their codes of morals, the rights of rulers and subjects, their hopes and fears of a future life, have all been the outcome of their conception of the universe. Their whole practical life has been the simple result of their theory of the origin of things. (Carlyle has said, "Tell me what a man thinks of this universe, and I will tell you what his religion is.")

And how is it with Christendom today? The popular conception of the nature and attributes of God, the nature of man, the origin and nature of evil; the practical questions of sin; the ecclesiastical schemes of salvation, heaven and hell; the prevailing theories of government and of social progress; the status of woman; the rights of children—all the great practical questions of humanity are the direct outgrowth of the Mosaic cosmogony, the Jewish theory of the origin of the universe. And the present condition, together with the past battles and progress of science, is the natural result of this same cause. Not practical, or of present importance? There is not a single question of the age, that for present, practical, pressing importance, begins to approach the one that Spencer and Darwin and Haeckel have raised. You might as well say that because the sun is ninety-two million miles away, its influence, and the laws of its life and shining, are of no practical importance to Boston. Boston is an outgrowth of the sunshine, from the granite that paves its streets to the brains that rule in its counsels. So the present active world, with all its widespread and multiplied interest, is the outgrowth of the far-off origin of things.

To specialize a little more particularly, and let you see how intimately religion is connected with the theory of the world, I ask you to look at the Church of the last two thousand years. Please observe that the whole orthodox system is the natural and logical outgrowth of the Mosaic account of the beginning of things in Genesis. The prevailing beliefs about God, the nature and fall of man, total depravity, the need and the schemes for supernatural redemption, the whole structure, creed, and ritual of the Church, the common belief about the nature and efficacy of prayer-meetings, the whole system of popular revivals, limited salvation and everlasting punishment—every single one of them is built on the foundation of the Mosaic cosmogony. And there is not one of them all but will be destroyed or modified when it shall become popularly settled that the Mosaic cosmogony is not a correct account of the facts.

Having made it appear, then, that as practical, earnest men of to-day, it is well worth our while to look into and investigate this question, I now ask you to go with me to a consideration of the only theories that need detain us. Of course we need not stop even to glance at the fantastic notions that prevailed among so many nations in the childhood of the world. Only two theories, the Mosaic and the Evolution, even pretend to claim the sober belief of our nineteenth-century civilization. To these, then, we must confine our attention.

The Mosaic Cosmogony

Before going any further, I wish to make two or three remarks that are worth careful attention.

(1) The account of creation in Genesis holds its place in the popular belief, not because it has been proved, or is capable of proof, but solely because of its supposed necessary connection with the truths of Christianity. This is, at any rate, a strange and questionable basis on which to found a scientific belief.

(2) It is an old-world traditional belief, not for the first time revealed to Moses, but one that came down from a time long before the foundation of the Hebrew nation.

(3) It does not even claim to be the result of a study of the facts that it proposed to explain. No such study was then possible, or had even been attempted; so that Moses is not telling what either he or any one else at that time had any way of knowing. It is only the traditional belief of that age.

(4) These traditions get a great deal of hardly deserved reverence and belief from the fact of their high antiquity; just as a man is proud of his ancestry, though the roots of his family-tree run down into outright barbarism. But, if you'll think of it, the reverence belongs here. We are the real ancients. The present is the hoary antiquity of the earth. 'Tis a man's old age, and not his childhood, that wears wisdom and gray hairs. This story of Moses is one of the fancies of the world's childhood. Never was civilization so old, and never had it such stores of accumulated knowledge, as now. In fact, never, until within the last hundred years, has the world gathered enough about the facts of the universe, so that mankind was competent to frame a reasonable theory of the world out of its acquired knowledge. If, then, in the history of humanity, there has ever been a time when there was a possibility of settling this question, now is that time.

(5) The Mosaic cosmogony has no scientific claim to be called a theory at all; for the simple reason that it explains nothing whatever. Its very claim to be an explanation is merely a leap into the incomprehensible. It simply says, "God made it." But that does not at all explain the method of creation—how, by what process, and according to what laws and forces, things have come to be as they are. I do not explain the mystery of life when I tell my child that God made the new baby, and that the angels brought it down to me. I do not explain a question in arithmetic when I tell a pupil that I worked it out and that so and so is the answer. But all these are explanations just as much as Genesis explains the world. Men seek the causes and the methods by which results have been produced. The solar system is explained by the law of gravitation not by saying God or the angels make the planets move.

Thus it is perfectly safe to say that no one would think of resting in the Mosaic story, were it not supposed to be a part of their religion to do so. And evolution has been opposed, not because it could not give good reasons for itself, but because it has been regarded as hostile to the popular religion.

With these remarks, then, in mind, we are ready to look at Genesis. The popular belief has been simply this: God had lived alone, complete and happy in himself, from all eternity. Suddenly, for no conceivable reason, he concluded to create the world. Previously, however, he had made the angels, that they might serve and praise him; though what service or praise he needed, who was complete in himself, it were hard to tell. If he had any motive in creating the world, it was thought to be that he might glorify himself, and receive the admiration of his creatures. The chief result was to be, that, after the world had passed away, his goodness in saving a few, and his justice in damning the many, might be seen as the result of his scheme of redemption. When, then, he was ready, by the word of command, he created matter out of nothing, and of this matter built the world. This world, a flat surface, he anchored in the midst of space, "setting it fast forever, so that it could not be moved." Then he elaborated the solid concave arch of the firmament, and placed it like a dome over the earth. In this he arranged the sun, moon, and stars, to divide the seasons, the days, and the nights, and to give light to this earth. He separated the waters, making the oceans of that which he left on earth; and in his storehouses "above the firmament," he treasured up the rains to water the earth, which watering was to be done by opening the windows of the sky, and letting the water through. Then he made the different forms of life, creating fishes and reptiles, and birds and animals, out of the dust. When this is done, it occurs to the Deity that none of these creatures can think of or praise him: so he consults, and concludes to make man in his own image. He forms Adam out of the dust, and then breathes in his nostrils, and he becomes alive. Then, seeing he is lonesome, he concludes to make woman to keep him company. So he puts him to sleep, takes out one of his ribs—which, strange to say, has never been missed—and from it constructs Eve. All this has taken him six days. He is now tired, and gives one day to rest. This is the origin of the Sabbath. If by resting is meant letting creation alone, we should suppose it might have fallen into disorder during the neglect. But if it means simply ceasing to create, then he has been resting ever since, on this theory; and it is hard to see why it is stated that he took only one day. But we know now that the process of creation has never ceased: so that we can get no meaning out of it at all. Even Jesus declared that this Father was working still.

Now, it is not my intention to insult your intelligence by proving to you that this is not true. The conception of God and of his methods is such as the world's childhood might ignorantly imagine; but no free intellect of the present age cares even to refute it. Only to look at it is sufficient refutation. Genesis contains contradictory accounts even of the original creation; and the inspiration of the Old Testament was not such as to prevent the most palpable mistakes being made in describing natural things.

We may now pass on to consider:

The Theory of Evolution

It would transcend our limits to attempt even an outline of the proofs of this theory. These are to be found in the works of the masters of science, specially prepared for that purpose. I must, therefore, content myself with remarking some of the surface probabilities, and then placing the theory itself alongside the Mosaic, that you may compare them.

(1) It is a fact that ought to make men stop and think, before rejecting it, that almost every trained scientific man living, who is competent to give a judgment on the questions, is a believer in evolution. If all the skillful doctors were agreed about a certain disease, it would hardly be modest for us to say they were wrong. When all the generals are at one about a military question, the probabilities are decidedly their way. When all the architects agree about a building, and when all the painters unite in defense of a question in art, outsiders should at least hesitate. Nearly all the present opposition to evolution comes from theology; but theology does not happen to know anything about it. As though I should attempt to settle a disputed point in music by the sense of smell, or a case of color (red or white) by hearing! The men who oppose evolution may be generally divided into two classes—those actuated by theological prejudice, and those who know nothing about it.

(2) The theory of evolution is constructed out of the observed and accumulated facts of the universe: it is not guess-work. The men who have elaborated this answer to the old question, How did things come to be as they are? are men who have gone to the facts themselves, and asked the question. They went to the earth and studied it and so developed the science of geology; they looked at the stars to see how they moved, and so made astronomy; they studied animals to see how they grew, and so made zoology; they studied man, and so made physiology and anthropology. If anybody, then, in the world, has any right to an opinion on the subject, it is those who have looked at the facts to find out about them. And it is simply absurd to see people offer an opinion who have no better stuff than ignorance or prejudice to make it out of.

(3) It stands the very highest test of a good theory; that is, it takes into itself, accounts for, and adjusts, almost every known fact; while there is not one single fact known that makes it unreasonable for a man to be an evolutionist.

Now, what is the theory? Simply this: that the whole universe, suns, planets, moons, our earth, and every form of life upon it, vegetable and animal, up to man, together with all our civilizations, has developed from a primitive fire-mist or nebulae that once filled all the space now occupied by the worlds; and that this development has been according to laws and methods and forces still active, and working about us today. It calls in no unknown agency. It does not offer to explain a natural fact by a miracle which only deepens the mystery it attempts to solve. It says, "I accept and ask for only the forces that are going on right before my eyes, and with these I will explain the visible universe." Certainly a magnificent pretension, and, if accomplished, a magnificent achievement, of the mind of man.

Look at the theory a little more in detail. Evolution teaches that the space now occupied by suns and planets was once filled with a fire-mist, or flaming gas. This mist, or gas, by the process of cooling and condensation, and in accordance with the laws of motion naturally set up in it, in the course of ages was solidified into the stars and worlds, taking on gradually their present motions, shapes, and conditions. This is the famous "nebular hypothesis." In favor of this theory is the fact that the earth is now in precisely the condition we should expect it to be, on this supposition. The moon, being smaller than the earth, has now become cold and dead. Jupiter and Saturn, being larger, are still hot—halfway between the sun's flaming condition and the earth's habitable one. And then all through the sky are clouds of nebulae, still in the condition of flaming gas, whirling, and assuming just such shapes as the evolution theory alone can explain. The theory further teaches, that, when the cooling earth had come into such a condition that there were land and water and an atmosphere, then life appeared. But how? By any special act of creation? No. It introduces no new or unknown force, and calls for no miracle. Science discovers no impassable gulf between what we ignorantly call dead matter, and that which is alive. It does not believe any matter is dead: so it finds in it "the promise and potency of every form of life." It has discovered a little viscous globule, or cell, made up chiefly of nitrogen and albumen. It is a chemical compound, the coming into existence of which is no more wonderful than the formation of a crystal, and calls no more urgently for a miracle than a crystal does. This little mass, or cell, is not only the lowest and most original form of life, but it is the basis of every form. There is no single form of life on the globe, from the moss on a stone up to the brain of Sir Isaac Newton, that is not a more or less complex compound or combination of this primary, tiny cell; and there is no stage in the process of development, where ascertained laws and forces are not competent to produce the results. There is no barrier between the vegetable and animal kingdom. No naturalist living can tell where the one leaves off, and the other begins, so insensibly do they merge into each other, like day passing through twilight into night. Neither is there any barrier between species, either of plants or animals. This point is now settled. Evolution also (what no other theory does) explains the distribution of plants and animals over the surface of the earth. It explains the present condition of the races of mankind—the progress of some, the stagnation of others, and the cases of gradual decay and dying-out. It explains social, political, and religious movements and changes, rises and falls. It is gradually proving its capacity to grapple with and solve the great enigmas and questions of the ages. And when generally understood and accepted, it will modify and direct all the forces and movements of the modern world.

From the primeval fire-mist, then, until today, the world has grown, without any necessity for, or help from, special creations, miracles, or any other forces than those known and recognized as at work right around us. It has taken millions of years to do this; but what are they in eternity? There have been no cataclysms, nor breaks, nor leaps. The sun has shone, the rain has fallen, the winds have blown, the rivers have run, the oceans have worn the shores, the continents have risen and sunk, just as they are doing now; and all these things have come to pass.

But some will say, "This is blank and outright atheism. You have left God entirely out of the questions. Where has he been, and what has he been doing, all these millions of years? From the fire-mist until today, all has gone along on purely natural principles, and by natural laws, you say?" Yes, that is just what evolution says. But, before we call it atheism, let me ask you a question. Here is a century-old oak-tree. The acorn from which it sprung was the natural product of some other oak. It fell to the earth, and the young oak sprouted. From that day to this—a hundred years—the oak has simply grown by natural law. You want no miracle to explain it. Is your theory of the oak, then, atheistic? Is it any less strange that the oak should grow than that thousands of other oaks, and other forms of life, should do the same? When a child is born it grows, you say, by natural law. Is it any more wonderful that it should be born by natural law? (and that all life should be born, and should develop, by natural law?) You are just as atheistic to say that a tree or a child grows by natural law, as evolution is, when it says the world did the same. Suppose science should put its God back in the past some millions of ages, while Moses puts his back only six thousand years, would the difference in time make one theory more atheistic than the other? But I should call pushing him back six thousand years, or a hundred million years, or even five minutes, even, more atheistic than I should like to believe. So I would do neither the one nor the other. What if we see the life and power and movement of God in the fire-mist, in all the growing worlds, in the first appearance of life on the planet, in the forms that climb up through all grades to man? What if we see him in the dust of the street, in the grasses and flowers, in the clouds and the light, in the ocean and the storms, in the trees and the birds, in the animal, lifting up through countless forms to humanity? What if we see him in the family, in society, in the state, in all religions, up to the highest outflowerings of Christianity? What if we see him in art, literature, and science? What if we make the whole world his temple, and all life a worship? All this we may not only do in evolution, but evolution helps us do it. I shall be greatly mistaken if the radicalism of evolution does not prove to be the grandest of all conservatism in society and politics not only, but in religion as well. It will turn out to be the most theistic of all theisms. It will give us the grandest conception of God that the world has ever known. It is inconsistent with "orthodoxy," but not with religion. It is charged by the thoughtless with being materialistic; but in reality it is any thing else. It so changes our conception of matter as utterly to destroy the old "materialism." It not only does not touch any one of the essential elements of true religion, but, on the other hand, it gives a firm and broad foundation on which to establish it beyond the possibility of overthrow. To illustrate this will be the work of future treatment of the special topics.

It only remains for me now to suggest a comparison as to grandeur and divinity between the two theories of creation. So many thoughtless sneers have been flung at the theory that dared talk of man's relationship to the ape, that a comparison like this may help change the sneer to admiration.

We marvel at Watt, the first constructor of a steam-engine; but it has taken many a brain beside his to bring it to its present perfection. What if he had been able to build it on such a plan, and put into it such a generative force, that it should go on, through long intervals of time, developing from itself improvements on itself, until it had become adapted to all the need of man? It should fit itself for rails; it should grow into adaptation for country roads and city streets; it should swim the water and fly the air; it should shape itself to all elements and uses that could make it available for the service of man. Suppose that all this should develop from the first simple engine that Watt constructed and should do it by virtue of power that Watt himself implanted in it? The simple thought of such a mechanism makes us feel how superhuman it would be, and how worthy of divinity. Is it not infinitely more than the separate construction of each separate improvement? And yet this supposition is simplicity and ease itself, compared with the grand magnificence of creation after the Darwinian idea. Who can pick an acorn from the ground and, looking up to the tree from which it has fallen, try to conceive all the grand and century-grown beauty and power of the oak as contained in the tiny cone in his hand, and not feel overwhelmed by the might and the mystery of the works of God? How unutterably grander is the thought that the world-wide banyan-tree of life, with all its million-times-multiplied variety of form and function, and beauty and power, standing with its roots in the dust, and with its top "commercing with the skies," and bearing on its upper boughs the eternal light of God's spiritual glory, is all the godlike growth of one little seed in which the divine finger planted such fructifying force!

A Story Big Enough to Hold Us All

Michael Dowd

The publication of *On the Origin of Species* marked a turning point in human history. New truths no longer spring fully formed from the traditional founts of knowledge. Rather, they are hatched and challenged in the public arena of science. For the first time, an understanding of reality is emerging that draws on the talents and insights of individuals of all ethnicities, all religious traditions, and all regions of the globe. We have a story of ancestry and shared inheritance that is big enough to include us all. This great story of humanity, life, and the universe reaches back billions of years, and offers vital guidance for living today and into the future.

A story big enough to hold us all depends entirely on the modern method by which we access and expand our understanding of reality. Science offers an entirely new means for acquiring the foundational knowledge from which diverse meanings can be drawn. This is the realm of *public revelation*. In contrast, *private revelation* entails claims about reality that arise primarily from personal experiences —some of which can be compelling. But private revelations enshrined for centuries in sacred texts cannot be empirically verified today. Such claims cannot be proven because they are one-person, one-time occurrences, obscured by the passage of time. When private revelations reside at the core of religious understandings, people are left with the choice to either believe them or not. And here lies the great problem of religion in the modern world.

We can distinguish public from private revelation by contrasting the approaches of Charles Darwin and Alfred Russel Wallace —the two men who independently discovered the concept of "evolution by natural selection." The latter is almost unknown today outside academic biology and the history of science. Indeed, Wallace himself demurred to the elder Darwin as the one who should be regarded as the originator of the theory. He deferred to Darwin to such a degree that in 1889 (seven years after Darwin's death) Wallace published his response to criticisms of the theory of evolution by natural selection—and titled it *Darwinism.*

The idea of evolution—then usually referred to as "transmutation of species"—had been discussed by scientists for more than half a century before 1858, when Darwin and Wallace unveiled their shared idea of *how* it takes place. Although the notion that species change over time and are intimately related to each other was tantalizing, the long-held and easily understood explanation that "God did it" did not have a robust competitor until a natural process could be identified and evidence amassed to support it.

Darwin and Wallace independently offered the same explanation: that the sum total of living and nonliving pressures in the natural world would, in effect, "select" among variations that from time to time naturally occur within species. Those individuals less capable of surviving and reproducing within their environment would leave fewer offspring, while those whose variations made them more capable of surviving and reproducing would leave more offspring. Over time, the character of the species as a whole would shift, as the more successful variations accumulated and prevailed. Despite the uncanny similarity in their respective ideas, Darwin and Wallace differed profoundly in how (and when) each chose to offer his new theory to the world.

As evidenced from Darwin's notebooks, the idea of transmutation of species by means of natural selection came to him gradually. Over the course of twenty years Darwin not only ruminated on the idea but tested it—searching for evidential support and carefully considering the kinds of evidence that, if discovered, would falsify the theory. Though he was secretive about his theory during its development—sharing it in bits and pieces with only his most trusted colleagues—he nevertheless drew vital assistance from the entire population of fellow naturalists. Housebound by chronic illness (and perhaps by disposition), he nonetheless corresponded often and on a wide range of topics with his colleagues. In particular, he requested reports of observations and biological specimens that helped support or refute his grand theory. *On the Origin of Species* is filled with references to these correspondences.

In contrast, although Alfred Russel Wallace had read many of the same papers and books that Darwin had, the idea of transmutation of species came to him in a flash. According to his autobiography, Wallace was suffering from an attack of fever on a remote Indonesian island when revelation struck. He immediately sent a brief description of his theory to Darwin and requested that he consider passing it on to the premier naturalist of their time, Charles Lyell. This correspondence forced Darwin's hand. His time was up. He would now have to make public his own writings on the topic, so that his and Wallace's work could be published in the same journal at the same time. Darwin then feverishly began working on a much longer piece to be published the next year, 1859—*On the Origin of Species by Means of Natural Selection.*

Wallace's flash of insight was a private revelation. Any such insight—whether occurring to Wallace or Moses, Einstein or Mohammed, Friedrich Kekule or Joseph Smith—however personal it may seem, is born from the riches of personal experience, previous ruminations, and exposure to ideas circulating in the culture. Thus private revelation sometimes heralds new scientific theories, just as it heralds new religious proclamations. But there is a huge difference between private and public revelation in what happens to the insight over time.

In scripturally based religions, private revelation at some point is codified in written form that carries into the future. Often the written form itself is accorded reverence and literal interpretation, which can lead to its use as justification for attitudes and actions out of sync with the shifting values of evolving cultures and technologies. In contrast, private revelations within science maintain no purchase—no matter how revered the author—unless the ideas offer fruitful ways to understand the natural world. Especially as new technologies such as telescopes, microscopes, and computers provide new opportunities for data gathering and analysis, private insights in science will be consigned to the dustbin if they do not eventually become public revelation—that is, part of humanity's growing collective intelligence.

Not uncommonly in science, a flash of insight sets the course for an extended period of research, testing, and writing, followed by submission to a journal, peer review, responses to peer review, and finally (if successful) publication. This is only the first phase, however. Rarely is any new idea launched in a journal such that every scientist active in that field is convinced. The naysayers set about trying to prove the theory wrong. Even after a theory garners enough evidential support to be regarded as factual, decades or centuries later new discoveries may force substantial modifications upon it—or even overturn it.

Alfred Russel Wallace ceded from the outset that Charles Darwin had amassed far more evidence in support of the theory of natural selection than he had. Steeped in the methodologies of empirical science, Wallace knew that, while private revelations were important, what made any idea worthy was the degree to which it made sense of the world—and was supported by solid evidence. The next threshold for an idea is the extent to which it inspires one's colleagues to add their own supportive evidence and to perform additional tests to support or refute the theory. The final test is whether the theory makes predictions or inspires new ideas that likewise prove useful, perhaps in very different areas of inquiry.

Few things contribute more to inter-religious acrimony and violence than the tendency to selectively embrace the technological fruits of public revelation while ignoring or disparaging the knowledge base that produces those technologies. That tension is unlikely to be resolved until a further distinction is made between what I like to call "day language" and "night language." *Day language* describes the realm of what's so: the facts, the objectively real, that which is publicly and measurably true. *Night language* evokes the realm of meaning in inspiring ways. It does so by way of metaphor, poetry, and vibrant images. This side of our experience is subjectively real, like a nighttime dream, though not objectively real. Night language is personally or culturally meaningful. It nourishes us with compelling images of emotional truth.

The language we use really does make a difference. Our choices of metaphors shade our experience of reality in a particular way. We will always make events or circumstances mean something. Even if we say something is meaningless, we're making it mean nothing. Humans swim in a sea of meaning no less than fish swim in water. We cannot avoid it. Problems arise when we fail to distinguish the factual, objectively real from the meaningful, subjectively realistic—when we mistake our interpretations for what's so. The two are not the same. Facts are delimited; interpretations are manifold.

Building on the distinction between public and private revelation, we can say this: Private revelation is grounded in subjective experience and is expressed in traditional, or religious, night language. Public revelation is grounded in objective experience; it is measurable and verifiable, and is expressed in day language.

Whenever we think or talk about an event, there is always what happened, the story about what happened, and the meaning we make out of the story of what happened. "What happened" refers to the uninterpreted, measurable, objective facts—the raw data. "The story about what happened" is the narrative context we consciously or unconsciously weave to connect the dots. Central to the story are the cause-and-effect linkages we effortlessly make from a stream of undifferentiated data. As language-using animals, we create stories as instinctually as we seek food when we're hungry. "The meaning we make out of what happened" is even more subjective. It entails all the things we tell ourselves and others about how we interpret the story of what happened—that is, what we make the story mean about us, others, and the world.

A source of anguish and conflict between individuals, between religions, and among nations is the consistent and near universal tendency to confuse the story about what happened and/or the meaning we make of it with what actually happened. We assume that what actually happened is both our story about what happened and also what we make that story mean. But truth is never our story, nor our interpretations, but only the measurable facts. The further we move from day language into night language, the greater the disagreements.

We cannot solve the problems posed by night language disagreements by jettisoning that facet of reality. We need both day and night language in order to have a meaningful experience of life. The important thing is to get the order right. If we first seek clarity on the measurable facts—the very mission of science—the night language stories and expressions of meaning that derive from those facts can enrich our lives and support cooperation across ethnic and religious differences. Basing or reinterpreting all our night expressions on a solid foundation of factual, public revelation is our best chance for achieving harmonious relationships at all levels.

What is remarkable about the concept of evolution is the degree to which Darwin's 1859 treatise has withstood the test of time. Nonetheless, it would be against the grain of science to call him a prophet or to judge the merit of his claims by the strengths and weaknesses of his character. Yet it is disconcerting how often scriptural literalists want to argue against evolution based on a 150-year-old book. This is why it is important to distinguish between the realms of public and private revelation—and why it is crucial that our religious traditions have the opportunity to evolve as much as science does. This may mean that certain religious people need to face some uncomfortable questions. For example:

Is it true that the entire universe literally was created in six days, as suggested in the first chapter of Genesis? Today millions of people believe so—and millions do not. The result on a personal level is families sundered by theological differences. The result collectively is intense conflict over the teaching of science in America's public schools.

Is it historically real that God intentionally drowned billions of animals and tens of millions of human beings in Noah's flood and instructed Moses to kill millions of men, women, and innocent children, as the Bible says (Genesis 6–9; Exodus 32:27–28; Deuteronomy 2:34, 3:4–5, 7:1–2; Joshua 11:12–15)? Countless people believe that these stories reveal God's unchanging moral character. Countless others believe they do not. The personal result: millions who leave their religious traditions, unable to worship such a God. The collective result: warring nations, each convinced that God is on its side.

Is it in fact the case that devout Jews and Christians will burn forever in hell because they do not embrace as the word of God the teachings of the prophet Muhammad, as recorded in the Qur'an? Hundreds of millions of Muslims believe this is so. And hundreds of millions of non-Muslims (as well as many liberal Muslims) don't. The personal result: good people who come to harbor judgment and resentment against other good people, as well as heartache and estrangement between family members who hold differing beliefs. The collective result: communities and nations divided.

These are among the conundrums promoted by worldviews based on private revelation, embedded in unchangeable scripture. They are by their very nature irresolvable. That is, short of worldwide conversion to one belief system or worldwide expulsion of all belief systems, the future of humanity will continue to be compromised by adversities born of conflicting beliefs—especially in a world in which weapons of mass destruction now come in small packages.

In contrast, the arena of public revelation offers us opportunities to learn ever more about the nature of reality—and to recognize and revise mistaken notions. People of all philosophical and religious backgrounds can agree on the same basic understandings, regardless of how those understandings will be interpreted. All reli-

gions and worldviews already contribute some of their most inquis-
itive, capable, and devoted citizens to the now-planetary effort of
public revelation—otherwise known as the scientific endeavor.

The mindset that welcomes public revelation is marked not
only by openness and curiosity. It is grounded in a trust so solid
that nothing that might be revealed would shake its foundation.
What is this trust? Here is mine: I have faith in the God-given ability
of myself and others—individually and especially collaboratively
—to interpret any new discovery made in any of the sciences in
lifegiving ways that serve the whole. Lifegiving interpretation is
key because the science versus religion wound in American society
will continue to fester so long as scientists and evolutionists keep
perpetuating the wrongheaded notion that science necessarily
yields a meaningless or depressing worldview—saying, "that's just
the way it is." From this perspective, those who see in evolution no
reason for hope are said to be realists. Those who are inspired by
or imagine the future of the world through evolution are said to be
wishful thinkers or simply out of touch with reality. Interestingly,
atheists and fundamentalists generally agree on this. But both are
demonstrably wrong.

Is it possible to focus on certain aspects of evolution and find
little, if anything, to get excited about—little that anyone would be
inclined to call gospel or good news? Absolutely. This is especially
true if one ignores long-term evolutionary and cultural trends.
But it is also possible, and certainly far more useful, to highlight
those aspects of the history of the universe, including human history, that provide inspiration and offer realistic hope for humanity
and all life.

Scientists can tell us what is and what was and, to some extent,
what will be. But they cannot tell us what it all means. For example, Big Bang cosmology is almost universally accepted within
science. Yet, it is up to each of us to choose whether we feel welcome or alien in that sort of universe and what that means for our
religious and spiritual perspectives. Past bards of the evolutionary
epic sometimes presented the story as a quest. The Jesuit mystic

and paleontologist Pierre Teilhard de Chardin told the story as life "groping" toward a kind of Christic unification. Others, notably the evolutionary biologist Julian Huxley, wove a tale of life emerging step by step, with no goal in sight, no lure beckoning. Philosopher Daniel Dennett's metaphor can help us distinguish between these two worldviews. He compares Huxley's epic to the construction of a skyscraper from the ground up using "cranes," or earthly processes. Teilhard's story is more like a building being lifted by "skyhooks," the pull of a higher spiritual force. Both tellers are challenged to offer an emotionally satisfying picture and to evoke a sense of belonging without compromising truth.

Any instructive telling of a story big enough to hold us all must include an interpretive meaning, but one that is nuanced with regard to how that meaning comes about. Four hundred million years ago, when an ancient lobe-finned fish set out across a tidal flat in desperate search of water, it had no inkling that its effort would ultimately lead to feathered flight and cathedrals. Foresight is foreign to the pre-human evolutionary process. Thanks to a big brain, however, our species has the extraordinary gift of hindsight. We can discern in the grand sweep of time a movement toward greater complexity and hence greater opportunity that was not available to a struggling fish—literally, out of water.

In hindsight, this one event prepared the way for something to come. Coincidence, even misfortune, was turned into opportunity. But we should remember that at the time of each new evolutionary development, the organisms involved hadn't a clue that anything grander might await their descendants. They were just looking for another tide pool. The heroes of the evolutionary epic have all been Forrest Gumps. And isn't that marvelous! This version of evolution, this version of "In the beginning" encourages us to entertain the possibility—the realistic possibility—that evolution is happening right now through us. More, what may feel like desperate fumblings could be the very stuff that launches the evolutionary epic across yet another threshold. Maybe you, maybe me, as individuals, right now, in our own little lives, have made some choice that will play out powerfully over the ages. Truly, this way of seeing our place in creation is invigorating.

Theologian Gordon Kaufman coined a striking term that reminds us of this fanciful, fluky aspect of the evolutionary epic. He calls the process underlying it all "serendipitous creativity." That puts us in partnership with the divine—not masters of our fate but partners, groping our way forward. What a difference it makes to be groping our way forward in faith—in partnership with God or, should you prefer less religious terminology, trusting the universe, trusting reality, trusting time.

The evolutionary epic as a sacred narrative that embraces yet transcends all scientific, religious, and cultural stories may eventually come to be cherished by the traditionally religious for enriching the depth and breadth of our experience of God. Our common creation story offers a refreshingly intimate, scientifically compelling, and theologically inspiring vision of God that can provide common ground for both skeptics and religious believers. These days, any understanding of God that does not at least mean "ultimate reality" or "the wholeness of reality" (measurable and non-measurable) is a trivialized and inadequate notion of the divine.

Reality as a whole is divinely creative in a way that we might describe as nested and emergent. Subatomic particles reside within atoms, which comprise molecules, cells, organisms, and societies —like nesting dolls of expanding size and complexity. Looking outward, we find planets within star systems, within galaxies, within superclusters of galaxies. Each of these is a *holon*—it is both a whole in its own right and a part of some larger whole. At every level, these holons express unique forms of divine creativity, powers that yield emergent novelty. For example, protons and other subatomic particles churning in the cores of stars fuse into most of the atoms in the periodic table of elements. In turn, hydrogen and oxygen atoms merge into molecules of water, with properties that transcend those of the parts. Together, the sun and the Earth bring forth fishes and forests, dragonflies and dancers. Finally, out of human cultures come art, music, religious theologies, and scientific theories. Thus, reality understood as "nestedly creative" is not a belief. It is an empirical fact (albeit expressed metaphorically) accepted by religious conservatives and atheists alike.

God, from this perspective, can be understood as a legitimate proper name for the largest nesting doll—the one and only creative reality that is not a subset of something larger. God is that which sources and infuses everything, yet is also co-emergent with and indistinguishable from anything. There are, of course, innumerable other ways one can speak about Ultimate Reality and theologize about God. But if God is not a rightful proper name for "the one and only creative reality that transcends and includes all other creative realities," then what is?

This way of thinking sheds light on traditional religious understandings of "God's immanence and transcendence." God is the wholly one, knowable and unknowable. God embraces, includes, and is revealed throughout the entire cosmos and in all of life. God is the great "I am" of existence. Yet as the source, energy, and end of everything, God cannot be limited to the world we can sense, measure, and comprehend; ultimate reality transcends and includes all that we can possibly know, experience, and even imagine.

This understanding of the divine mocks the question, "Do you believe in God?" Any God that can be believed in or not believed in is a trivialized notion of the divine. Like life, reality simply is—no matter what beliefs one may hold. What we choose to say *about* reality—the stories and beliefs we hold about its nature, purpose, direction, and so forth—is open for discussion, and differences among those choices are irresolvable. But who could deny that there is such a thing as "reality as a whole" and that God is a legitimate, though not a required, proper name for this ultimacy? The transparency of this point is surely one reason why this perspective garners the assent of many theists, atheists, agnostics, religious nontheists, pantheists, and panentheists alike.

When God is understood foundationally as a holy personification of "the wholeness of reality, measurable and nonmeasurable," everything shifts. New possibilities open for ways of thinking about creativity, intelligence, the universe, guidance, and our role in the evolutionary process.

Many among us have yet to cast off the belief that God spoke clearly and was actively involved in human affairs only in the distant past. Thankfully, there is a groundswell movement among Roman Catholics, mainline Protestants, Evangelicals, Mennonites, Quakers, Pentecostals, New Thought Christians, and others, who find glad tidings in the God-honoring ways of embracing a multi-billion-year story of evolutionary emergence—a story big enough and open enough to uplift the biblical stories within its compass. Thus we arrive, with reluctance or with great expectation, but nevertheless inevitably, at a threshold. To hold a literal interpretation of the Bible is to foster a schizophrenic break between the religion that still guides many of us and the science that improves so many aspects of our lives—including healing us from diseases, injuries, and birth defects that in other times would have been lethal. To continue to insist on a literal interpretation of the Bible in this age of science is to make an idol of human language, while underestimating both the extent of divine revelation and the depth of human fallibility.

We now know that it took many generations for the events described in the Bible to be recorded in written form. Yet today, by continuing to insist that ancient biblical texts are accurate records of the dictated words of an otherworldly, invisible father, we turn millions away from the real truths available in scripture. Adherence to literalism thus undermines the very gospel it seeks to support. Those who think that peoples of the past did not embellish stories to their own ends, and that these departures did not magnify over the decades and centuries of oral transmittal before being recorded in writing, do not understand human nature and the biblical portrayal of sin.

Although most Christians still call the collection of letters written two millennia ago the New Testament, the revolutionary idea today is that God has, for centuries, been faithfully and publicly revealing truth via facts uncovered by science. Perhaps we should call sacred interpretations of science the Ever-Renewing Testament.

The words of Philip Hefner, a Lutheran theologian and a leader in the religion and science dialogue, serve as a fitting conclusion. During his masterful presentation at a 1997 Epic of Evolution conference, he said:

> I like to think of our challenges as weaving. We are all weavers. The weaver constructs the warp, anchoring it to the loom, and then, by working the weft in and through the warp, creates patterns and the entire tapestry. The Epic of Evolution, in scientific form, is the warp on which all present and future meaning for our lives must be woven. There is no single correct way in which the weaving will take shape, no single authorized manner in which the Epic must appear in our worldviews. All of the various weavers of meaning will find something common in the warp. In the cultural crises that face us all, each will learn from how others move within the loom's constraints and possibilities. We humans are the cultural religious animals of evolution on our planet. We are here to weave the spiritualities that are life-giving for our phase of the Epic of Evolution and for the next generation.

Thanks to an evolutionary understanding of history and deep time, I now enjoy all the benefits and blessings of my Christian tradition from a place of knowledge rather than belief. That is, the cosmological understandings born of science are the ground on which core Christian concepts come alive for me and guide my path in this world.

GRANDEUR IN THIS VIEW

WILLIAM R. MURRY

In his autobiography, which at his request and out of respect for his wife's Christian faith, was not published until after his death, Charles Darwin wrote of his gradual conversion from belief to agnosticism. As a young man he had thought seriously about becoming an Anglican clergyman, and he writes that when he went aboard the *Beagle* in 1831 he thought of himself as a Christian. However, he notes that over the years "disbelief crept over me at a very slow rate but was at last complete." In the same work, he refers to the idea of the eternal punishment of non-Christians as a "damnable doctrine." He then refutes the traditional argument from design by replacing it with natural selection and argues against the immortality of the soul on naturalistic grounds. He also contends that the degree of evil and suffering in the world throws doubt on the idea of an omnipotent and loving deity, and since he can find no reason to believe in a divine creator, he remains "agnostic" on the matter.

There is no question that the discovery of evolution by natural selection has important implications for theology and religious belief. At the most obvious level, it undermines a literal interpretation of the Genesis account of creation by eliminating the need for a supernatural being who creates plants, animals, and human beings in finished form, similar to the way humans create useful artifacts or works of art. At the next level, it throws doubt on the notion of divine purpose in creation, the idea that God had a purpose in everything He created. The theory of natural selection maintains that the only purposes of organisms are to survive and reproduce. And finally, it questions whether a supernatural creator is necessary at all.

Despite the claims of creationists and those advocating intelligent design, the evidence for evolution is overwhelming. Evolution by natural selection is one of the two or three most important discoveries not only in the history of science but in the history of the world because it has changed our understanding of how we came to be, what we are, and our place in the world. It is at least as important, if not more so, as the discoveries of Copernicus and Einstein. However, just as it took several hundred years for the full implications of the Copernicus model of the solar system to be felt, so also all the implications of Darwin's idea have not yet become fully apparent.

Before Darwin, species were seen as fixed entities, creations of a deity who made them in the exact form in which we find them today. After Darwin, however, we understand that all living things have evolved over hundreds of millions of years from single-cell organisms that emerged in a kind of primal soup and learned to replicate themselves. After Darwin we know that we humans are all connected and are part of a great family tree stretching back across billions of years to the dawn of life. And most importantly, Darwin showed that human beings are as much a part of nature as trees and tigers, as beetles and beavers, with a lineage that includes countless diverse ancestors. Darwin destroyed the idea that human beings were a special creation made in the image of the deity. We may be unique—with consciousness and our ability to reason—but we are so because this uniqueness evolved, not because it was bestowed on us by a divine being.

Before Darwin we humans thought of ourselves, as the psalmist once described, as "a little less than God," or according to another translation, "a little lower than the angels," and infused with an immortal soul. The notion of Plato, Descartes, and most of Christian theology that human beings consist of an immortal soul temporarily housed in a transient physical body no longer makes sense. If we are, as evolution suggests, wholly natural beings rather than part natural and part supernatural, then the whole Christian construct of immortality, divine creation, and human beings made in the image of God crumbles.

By maintaining that we humans are created "in the image of God" Christianity has held that we have some of the same qualities as the divine, such as free will, the ability to love and forgive, to think and reason, and to act morally as beings who know the difference between right and wrong.

Evolution by natural selection, however, tells us that we consist of the same physical, chemical, and biological elements and structures as other living things. As Darwin claims in *On the Origin of Species*, "The structure of every organic being is related, in the most essential yet often hidden manner, to that of all other organic beings. . . . All living things have much in common, in their chemical composition, their germinal vesicles, their cellular structure, and their laws of growth and reproduction." The idea, held by many in the Western world since Plato, that we human beings consist of an eternal soul temporarily residing in a physical body, is now highly problematic. Neuroscience has shown that what we think of as a soul, our intelligence and emotions, consists of the multitudinous activity of trillions of neurons and synapses in our brain. One of the offspring of Darwinian evolution is cosmic evolution, which tells us that we are transformed stardust. As Michael Dowd describes it in *Thank God for Evolution*, we are "stardust that has evolved to the place that it can now think about itself and tell its own story."

If then, as Darwinian evolution teaches us, we are animals— albeit with the largest, most complex, and highly developed brains—then our reasoning is less reliable than we thought, our behavior is less free, and our loving and forgiving are more tied to our self-interest. We are not as special as we once supposed. We are simply the most highly evolved symbol-using animal that natural selection has produced. Darwin himself noted that "only our natural prejudice, and that arrogance which made our forefathers declare that they were descended from demi-gods" leads us to object to the idea that we are descended from other primates. But he predicted in *The Descent of Man* that, before long, people would wonder how naturalists who were familiar with the comparative structure of "man and other mammals should have believed that each was the work of a separate act of creation."

Thus evolution by natural selection has resulted in what might be called "radical naturalization" both in our self-understanding and in our understanding of the world. Among other things, Darwin's idea gave birth to evolutionary biology and evolutionary psychology, which have added considerably to our knowledge of how human beings evolved, how our brains work, and why we behave as we do. Darwin took our focus from the heavens to the earth. We now seek to understand ourselves in relationship to our evolutionary biological origins rather than our divine origins.

That does not mean we are not individuals of great worth and dignity. Unitarian minister William Ellery Channing writes in his 1828 sermon, "Likeness to God": "I do and must reverence human nature. . . . I shut my eyes on none of its weaknesses or crimes. I understand the proofs by which disposition demonstrates that man is a wild beast. . . . But injured, trampled on, and scorned as our nature is, I still turn to it with immense sympathy and strong hope." We have evolved with the capacities of love, self-consciousness, intelligence, creativity, courage and empathy, however, flawed or imperfect these may be.

Before Darwin, belief in an omnipotent divine being seemed self-evident in the Western world. Not so any more, and it is no wonder that religious conservatives are so strongly opposed to the teaching of evolution. They understand its implications. They know that it undercuts their most fundamental beliefs about God and human beings.

Recent research, cited by Gregory Paul in his article "The Big Religion Questions Finally Solved," has shown a correlation between belief in evolution and atheism or agnosticism. In the democracies of western Europe, including Scandinavia, the vast majority of people accept evolution and are unbelievers, while in the United States the majority reject evolution and are theists. In western Europe belief in evolution averages over 75 percent while belief in God is less than 25 percent on average. In the U.S. about 45 percent believe in evolution and over 80 percent believe in a supernatural God.

Does this mean that we can no longer believe in God? Not necessarily, but it does mean that our conception of divinity changes. It is now more difficult to think of God as a personal supernatural being who is omnipotent, omniscient, and the creator of all things, as Western theology has long maintained. Thus, many liberal theologians now conceive of God as a power and force within the natural universe, rather than a source outside it. Such a "naturalistic theism" has different expressions but usually affirms that God is not omnipotent in the sense of being coercive. Rather, the divine has a power of persuasion, not coercion. To some of these thinkers God is a force like a magnet drawing us toward goodness and health. All language about God is necessarily symbolic or metaphorical, and different images of God, such as Paul Tillich's "ground of being" can be helpful. This metaphor suggests that God is the life in which all things are rooted and from which all things draw nourishment and sustenance.

A naturalistic concept of God avoids some of the traditional criticisms leveled at supernatural concepts of divinity. A supernatural God, especially one who is symbolized as a father, tends to be authoritarian, issuing commandments, demanding obedience, and eliciting fear from his followers. Such a God tends to be strict, has an unyielding moral code, and punishes those who disobey. And as George Lakoff has argued in *Moral Politics*, people who believe in that kind of God tend to have families in which the father's word is law, children fear their parents, and disobedience is severely punished. They also tend to want a society with a strong military; severe punishment for criminals, including the death penalty; an understanding that a woman's place is in the home; and and consensus that homosexuality is immoral. The supernatural God is also depicted as male, which justifies a patriarchal society and discrimination against women, who are regarded as inferior.

Naturalistic theism, on the other hand, tends to symbolize God in more feminine terms—like Mother Nature more loving, less punitive, and less judgmental than "God the Father." People who believe in this kind of God tend to raise their children in a more nurturing, caring environment characterized by dialogue and cooperation. They favor a society that emphasizes peace and justice and negotiation in international matters. Humans are symbolic animals, and the symbols we associate with a deity make a lot of difference.

The theory of natural selection added considerably to the already mounting doubts about the necessity of a supernatural deity. These doubts began with Copernicus's revelation that the earth was not the center of the universe and were reinforced by geologists' discovery that the earth was at least millions of years old. Doubts increased as a result of early nineteenth-century Biblical scholarship, and grew stronger still with the Enlightenment's insistence on reason and empirical evidence as the way to truth.

Before Darwin, many scientists believed that science pointed to God as the first cause, the creator of the laws of nature, and the being who designed the world and its many complex inhabitants. Although not a scientist, William Paley, in his 1802 book *Natural Theology*, set forth the argument most scientists claimed. He argued that, just as a complicated mechanism like a watch required a watch maker, the universe with its incredible diversity and complicated organisms had to have had a creator. The argument from design was thought for many years to be the strongest argument for the existence of a supernatural deity. Today's advocates of "intelligent design" still hold to that belief.

But by showing how the complexity of living things could arise from the process of natural selection, Darwin removed the need for a designer. In his essay "The Intellectual Crisis of Belief," historian James Turner writes, "The Darwinian hypothesis of natural selection explained two of the three great instances of divine activity in biology—the origin of species and the adaptation of animals and plants to their environment—without reference to God."

In addition, it was difficult to reconcile the idea of a loving, benevolent and all-powerful deity with the theory of natural selection, which included competition for survival, suffering, killing, and even extinction—what Alfred, Lord Tennyson described as "nature, red in tooth and claw." If God is good, Darwin forced us to ask, why would He choose such a cruel process for His creation?

At the very least, the theory of natural selection moved God from the center of human life and thinking to the fringes. Darwin's idea was not the sole cause of the rise of skepticism in the Western world, but it made a significant, and for some a decisive, contribution to that skepticism. For many, it was the last nail in the coffin of a supernatural deity.

There are three primary ways in which theologians and others have tried to resolve the conflict between traditional religion and scientific understanding. The first is to suggest that each is a different but valid way of understanding the world. According to this view, religion is concerned with spiritual matters and questions of the meaning and purpose of human life, while science deals with the material world and questions of how the world works and what it consists of. The late paleontologist Stephen Jay Gould names these "non-overlapping magisteria" in his book *Rocks of Ages*. We could call this approach *parallelism* because the two ways of looking at the world never intersect.

However, we cannot separate our thinking about religion and science into air-tight compartments. What we have learned about life and the world from modern science affects what we think about the meaning and purpose of our lives. Darwin's ideas influence our thinking about who we are, what our lives mean, and our ultimate destiny. Susan Jacoby writes in a *Washington Post* blog article,

"That so many manage to accommodate belief systems encompassing both the natural and the supernatural is a testament not to the compatibility of science and religion but to the flexibility . . . of the human brain."

A second approach to the relationship between religion and science is that of the religious fundamentalist, who denies the significance of science and rejects any scientific ideas that would jeopardize religious beliefs. While parallelism accepts scientific method and discoveries but denies their significance for religious belief, the conservative approach simply rejects the discoveries of science that seem to conflict with religious doctrine.

A third approach is for religion to learn from science and to adapt its convictions to what science has learned. Since modern scientific discoveries such as evolution by natural selection are part of our culture in the West, it is important to re-interpret religion in light of those discoveries and allow it to speak in the context of the contemporary worldview. The result is a dynamic religion that constantly learns from science, evolving new understandings and becoming a scientifically informed religious perspective. The alternative is a religion couched in the stories, myths, symbols, and doctrines of another era, which for many people have lost their meaning and power.

In the United States *On the Origin of Species* met with both positive and negative responses. Some scientists, such as Harvard botanist Asa Gray, argued that it was possible to accept evolution and remain a Christian because science and religion referred to two different kinds of truth. Others, such as geologist Louis Agassiz, rejected Darwin's idea because in his view it led to atheism.

Ministers and theologians also fell into both camps. On the positive side, both Ralph Waldo Emerson and Henry David Thoreau accepted it. In 1874 Rev. Minot Savage, Unitarian minister of the Church of the Messiah in New York City, published a book of sermons entitled *The Faith of Evolution,* which became a best seller under the 1876 title *The Religion of Evolution.* Noting that religion needs to adapt to the new discoveries of science if it is to remain vital, Savage pointed out that Christianity originally opposed other scientific advances that it now accepts and called on people of faith to embrace evolution as just such a breakthrough. The eminent liberal Protestant Henry Ward Beecher also believed that evolution was compatible with Christian faith. Freethinkers and agnostics like Elizabeth Cady Stanton and Robert G. Ingersoll of course embraced evolution as further proof that theistic religion was simply superstition. The theory also played an important role in the emergence of religious humanism, culminating in the publication of "The Humanist Manifesto" of 1933. Religious humanism was and is an effort to adapt religious beliefs to the discoveries of modern science.

The science vs. religion debate came to a head with the famous Scopes Trial in Dayton, Tennessee, in 1925, which illustrated both the split between the North and the South on the issue and the depth of feelings on both sides. In general, the more religiously conservative South rejected evolution and opposed any effort to reconcile it with Christianity while the North was predisposed to reconciliation.

The theory of evolution united human begins with other living things. Biologist George Wald explains that despite the great variety of life forms which have evolved over the millennia, their basic biological entities differ little. In his article "Theological Resources from the Biological Sciences" he writes,

> The biological cells which constitute a maple leaf, a caterpillar, and a human brain are basically the same in structure and components; the organisms have achieved different forms by organizing the cells in different patterns and calling upon them to perform different functions.

Biologists have become acutely aware of the kinship of all living organisms. The result is a sense of the unity of all things. On the one hand, this suggests that all human beings are brothers and sisters, members of one family, with far more in common than otherwise. The spiritual implication is that we should live together in love and caring, that we should be tolerant of our differences, and that we should be responsible to and for one another. But we are also related to all others forms of life. Physician Frederick Gilkey once said in a presentation,

> When I look into the eyes of a gorilla in the zoo, I don't see a dumb beast, but a cousin, a remote one, to be sure, but a genuine relative. Is it not a source of strength to see all life on this planet as profoundly, intimately, and truly related?

If we are one with all of the natural world then we have a moral responsibility to care for and preserve it. This sense is expressed by Shug in Alice Walker's novel *The Color Purple* when she says, "I knew that if I cut a tree, my arm would bleed." Darwin's idea provides a deep spiritual grounding for a strong environmental ethic as well as for a nature spirituality. The seventh Principle of the Unitarian Universalist Association, in affirming the "interdependent web of all existence of which we are a part," emphasizes this same insight. This sense of unity, of our deep and abiding connection with all life, is surely a spiritual experience.

One of the effects of the theory of evolution is to take away the focus on the supernatural and put it on the natural. In a post-Darwinian world the fecundity and diversity of the natural world evoke feelings of awe and mystery, often identified as religious emotions. Physicist Chet Raymo writes in *When God Is Gone, Everything is Holy*, "Darwin counted himself an agnostic, but in his reverence for the creative agency of nature, we should count him a devoutly religious man." When William James writes in *The Varieties of Religious Experience* of "a new sort of religion of Nature, which has entirely displaced Christianity from the thought of a large part of our generation," he refers to a "veneration of evolution." Science in general and evolution in particular evoked this discovery of spiritual meaning in the natural world. And the late Carl Sagan put it beautifully in *The Demon-Haunted World*: "When we recognize our place in an immensity of light years and in the passage of ages, when we grasp the intricacy, beauty, and subtlety of life, then that soaring feeling, that sense of elation and humility combined, is surely spiritual."

Adoration of nature was not new to the Western world. After all, the psalmist proclaims, "The heavens declare the glory of God and the firmament shows his handiwork." The early Christian nature mystics regarded the environment as a pathway to God, and Jonathan Edwards too found in the beauty of the natural world evidence of God's loving heart. Emerson, whose first published work was his great essay "Nature," found spiritual depth in communion with plant and animal life. Early in that piece he writes,

> If the stars should appear one night in a thousand years, how would men believe and adore; and preserve for many generations the remembrance of the city of God which had been shown! But every night come out these envoys of beauty, and light the universe with their admonishing smile. The stars awaken a certain reverence, because though always present, they are inaccessible, but all natural objects make a kindred impression, when the mind is open to their influence.

Evolution, with its insight into the long and arduous evolutionary journey of plants, animals, birds, fish, and human beings gave us a new way to understand the many miracles of nature. Just to look at a cat or a bird or a tree and to imagine how it came to be and how it acquired its marvelous abilities is enough to fill one's mind with astonishment. Or to contemplate the fact that the DNA in a single cell of our bodies, so small we cannot see it, if stretched out would reach from fingertip to fingertip of our outstretched arms and that there are trillions of cells in a body and that there is enough DNA in those cells to reach to the sun and back, can fill us with profound amazement.

Equally astonishing is the thought that a human body consists of 10 trillion cells and that a brain contains about 100 billion neurons and 100 trillion synapses. Even the power of nature, despite its potential destructiveness, can be a source of awe.

Every religion needs a story, and evolution has given us a story with multiple layers of rich meaning. It is the epic of cosmic and biological evolution. It is a religious story because it calls us out of our little self-centered worlds and enables us to see ourselves as part of the great living system we call the cosmos. This story gives a larger meaning and broader ethic to our lives. Our connection to nature is a profound spiritual experience that evokes our veneration.

The epic of evolution that begins with the big bang provides us with a vision of the universe as a single reality, one long spectacular process of development, an unfolding drama, a universal story for humankind—our story. Like no other, it humbles us as we contemplate the complexity of the cosmic process, and amazes us when we try to imagine its magnitude. Like no other story, it gives us a scientifically based cosmology that tells us how we came to be and what we are made of. In her essay, "Welcome to the Ecozoic Era," Amy Hassinger writes, "The basic elements of our bodies—carbon, calcium, iron—were forged inside supernovas, dying stars, and are billions of years old. We are, in fact, made of stardust. We are intimately related to the universe." Like no other story, it teaches us that we are all members of one family, sharing the same genetic code and a similar history. Like no other story, it gives meaning and purpose to human beings as the agents responsible for the current and future stage of evolution—psycho-social evolution. Like no other story, it provides the individual with a meaningful worldview and a sense of belonging to a larger process. Darwin's idea did not create a nature spirituality, but it increased its importance and gave it deeper meaning.

"The Wedge," a leaked strategy document of intelligent design advocates, suggests that proponents of intelligent design are not primarily concerned about the truth of evolution but about the idea that teaching it leads to moral relativism. As Nancy Pearcey, a contemporary supporter of intelligent design, puts it on the Center for Science and Culture website, "Darwinian evolution tells us not only where we came from but also what behavior is natural and normative for humans. . . . Teach kids they are animals, and they'll act like animals."

This view represents a misunderstanding of evolution in several ways. For one thing it seems to contend that "survival of the fittest" refers to survival by strength and brutality. In fact, it refers to the organisms that adapt best to their environments, that "fit" best. Secondly, it assumes that the "is" of nature can be translated into an "ought" in behavior. But teachers can explain that morality does not logically flow from evolutionary theory. Just because mutations in organisms are random does not means that human morality is random.

While evolutionary theory does not imply certain moral principles, in recent years evolutionary psychologists and anthropologists have shown that ethical values are based in the pre-moral feelings and behaviors of our evolutionary ancestors and in the social relations of early humans. Evolutionary psychology and cognitive neuroscience also show how our moral intuitions work, why they evolved, and how they are implemented within the brain. Apes, monkeys, dolphins, and whales exhibit behaviors that include cooperation, mutual aid, altruism, sympathy, peacemaking, and community concern. These pre-moral feelings and behaviors became part of our genetic heritage. In an *Atlantic Monthly* article titled "The Biological Basis of Morality," Harvard biologist E.O. Wilson argues that cooperativeness and empathy may be heritable because "cooperative individuals generally survive longer and leave more offspring," meaning that genes "predisposing people toward cooperative behavior would have come to predominate in the human population as a whole."

As human beings lived in groups—families, clans, tribes, and ultimately cities and states—it became clear, for example, that actions such as murder and theft endangered self-preservation, and prohibitions against them arose. In addition, these prohibitions, along with inherited traits like cooperation, evolved to become more inclusive. Moral values, like our physical organism, evolved over thousands of generations. They gradually developed from the human experience of living in societies, and they have both a biological and a social basis.

The late Unitarian Universalist minister John Ruskin Clark puts it well in his book *The Great Living System*:

> Norms of good and evil, of right and wrong, did not spring full-blown from somebody's head; they developed slowly over generations of trial and error. It is part of the mark of being human that we benefit from the experience of others. . . . To recognize that concepts of good and evil are derived from human experience is to give them a timeless validity. . . . The realization that morals are empirically grounded does not invalidate traditional norms, it greatly reinforces them.

Darwin himself saw that moral precepts were expanded and modified through thousands of generations, writing in *The Descent of Man*, "Any animal whatever, endowed with well-marked social instincts, the parental and filial affections being here included, would inevitably acquire a moral sense or conscience, as soon as its intellectual powers had become as well, or nearly as well developed as in man."

So although Darwinian theory does not suggest moral principles either implicitly or explicitly, it does help us understand their origins. This in turn helps to sever the supposed link between ethics and belief in God since it provides a naturalistic explanation for the origin and development of moral precepts and behavior. In *The Brothers Karamazov* by Dostoevsky, Ivan says that if God does not exist "all things are permitted." Evolutionary theory shows this is not the case, as does the existence of different forms of the Golden

Rule in non-theistic Confucian China, in the Stoicism of ancient Greece, and in other times and places. The question, "Can we be good without God?" can be answered, "Yes, people have been good without God for centuries"—just as some believers have been anything but moral.

It is not too much to say that *On the Origin of Species* changed everything. Darwin's theory revolutionized our understanding of ourselves, our sense of God and spirituality, our relationship to the natural world, and the origin and nature of morality. Far from resulting in a pessimistic or even nihilistic view of life, this brilliant theory leads to an understanding of what it means to be human that is both scientifically grounded and spiritually satisfying.

Making God's Work Our Own

John Gibbons

In 2005 I officiated at the memorial service of Dr. Ernst Mayr, the father of one of my parishioners and the leading evolutionary biologist of our era—"the Darwin of the twentieth century." Ornithologist, naturalist, and biologist, Dr. Mayr died at one hundred years of age, still thinking, still publishing, still finding things out until the very end. One cannot read anything about any aspect of biology or evolution without encountering him.

Dr. Mayr had left explicit instructions as to how he wished to be remembered. He said basically three things. He wished to be known as generous, giving his time and attention to students and colleagues. Generous also with the money he received for academic prizes which he gave to the causes of education and conservation. We may be generous, he said, because life is a generous giver—abundant, over-flowing, full of insight, beauty, and humor if we but look and see.

He asked also to be remembered as tolerant, that he had overcome—or strove to overcome—the racial, religious, and ethnic prejudices of his birth. Indeed, as new immigrants from Germany, he and his wife Gretel endured years of hardship and official suspicion before they were allowed passports and granted citizenship. He advised that all people be tolerant because the essence of life is difference and diversity, ebb and flow, chance and choice.

Third, Dr. Mayr asked that he be remembered for his appreciation of mystery and the unknown. He believed that in science, religion, and many things there's no point in speculating about things we do not or cannot know. In discussions and debates, he never made assertions about the Bible or any religion. He refused to entertain unanswerable questions. The island of knowledge, Mayr knew, is surrounded by a vast shoreline of mystery.

The memorial service touched on qualities recalled by others as well, including Mayr's ability to observe the world in the context of Darwinian "grandeur." He believed in looking and seeing and, like Darwin, was preeminently a realist, a believer in what *is*. As one of our naturalist poets, Mary Oliver, writes in "Look and See," "Oh (Life), how shinning and festive is your gift to us, if we / Only look, and see. . . ."

Mayr's realism was not an ethical neutrality but an ethical imperative, for it is we—not God or fate or life itself, but we—who bear all responsibility. This sense is reflected in the poem "In Praise of Feeling Bad About Yourself" by Wislawa Szymborska: "Among the signs of bestiality / A clear conscience is Number One."

The power and richness of Dr. Mayr's life touched and touches us all, and will continue to influence us well into the future. He lived Darwin. Through Mayr's passion and truth we learn more about Darwin and his passion and truth; why we should always remain curious about what is on the other side of the fence and why evolution still matters.

Evolution has been breaking news since the 1859 publication of Darwin's *On the Origin of Species*. It continues to be a radical scientific theory and fact, with startling religious implications. Do you ever recall being intrigued by the concept of a "universal acid," something that might eat through everything with which it comes in contact? If such an acid should exist, what could ever contain it? Evolution has been called a universal acid that eats through all the static ideas about life. It especially eats through all orthodox religious concepts of how life came into existence and what its purpose may be. It is difficult to overestimate the revolutionary

JOHN GIBBONS 47

import of Darwin and his theory. The publication of *Origin* marks the beginning of secular science; all earlier science made religious assumptions about life's origins and purpose.

Evolutionary thinking has had momentous consequences. A basic description of evolution by natural selection might help. Understand that the term *evolution* alone is not an adequate description; things might evolve for various reasons. Perhaps a supernatural God might direct evolution. The church evolves; governments evolve; video games and Volkswagens and dance styles evolve over time. In such cases humans, not God, bear responsibility. When we say "evolution by natural selection," however, we are saying that the changes that occur over time happen neither by divine nor human intervention but naturally, without external or fore-ordained purpose.

Evolution by natural selection occurs when the following three conditions are met: There is a population of things that make copies of themselves, the copying process is not perfect, and the copying errors lead to differences in the ability of offspring to survive and make copies of themselves. These conditions apply to animals and plants but also to anything that can copy itself. Computer viruses can copy themselves and, therefore, they too may evolve by natural selection.

A classic example of natural selection is of pale-white butterflies that once lived in an English forest. Their population increased because, sitting on pale tree branches, birds could not spot them easily. Then a smoke-belching factory was built near the forest. Pollution darkened the tree branches; the pale butterflies stood out against the branches and the birds feasted. But butterflies are a population that makes copies of themselves and the copying process is not perfect. So, occasionally—just by chance—butterflies were born that were even more pale than their parents and they were gobbled up even more quickly than the others. And yes, occasionally—by pure chance—some butterflies were also born who were more grey than their parents and so blended into the polluted tree branches. These lived to a ripe old age and had lots of offspring. After several generations, almost every butterfly in the forest was grey.

Pre-Darwinian scientists would likely have concluded that God, "the intelligent designer," made grey butterflies that gave camouflage against their predators. The difficulty with that view, though, is that that same God would have to have been responsible for the even more pale butterflies that attracted predators.

The ultimate purpose or function of an adaptation is not pre-determined. The feathers on birds seem to have their origins not to aid in flight but as a means of dispersing heat away from the animal's body. Those with feathers not only avoided overheating but were also less likely to get hurt—they had a little cushion if they chanced to fall out of a tree. Gliding came first, then flying. Something can evolve for one purpose, then acquire another; each step an improvement, but not every step serving the same purpose.

In contrast to pre-Darwinian scientists who compared God's creation to that of an intelligent watchmaker, British zoologist Richard Dawkins describes the process of natural selection as that of a "blind watchmaker." In his book with that title, he writes, "Unlike a real watchmaker, who plans out the watch he will make before he starts, natural selection aimlessly tinkers with organisms in a piecemeal fashion, with no particular end in sight."

There are revolutionary and liberal religious values inherent in this idea. First of all, the universal acid of Darwinism utterly disproves the notion that there is any one perfect or unchanging type of any species. Ernst Mayr, when asked what delayed the acceptance of evolution by natural selection, cited Western platonic philosophy —an idealism held by Plato and Aristotle, through Linnaeus and Mill, that there are ideal types or kinds of organisms: the quintessential perfect rabbit, woodpecker, butterfly, tree, white-handed gibbon monkey, or human being. In his work, Mayr reminded us that, like birds and flowers and all living things, we are each unique individuals, constituents of a multi-faceted population.

Mayr advised that we must adopt "population thinking." That is, we are a population of diverse individuals. In any biopopulation, no two individuals, not even identical twins, are actually identical. There is no such thing as the perfect ideal, unless you consider all to be perfect ideals (though its probably wiser to assume universal imperfection). Mayr debunked typological thinking—the origin of all prejudices. The failure to adopt population thinking is the primary source of racism, sexism, heterosexism, ableism, and ageism. January 2005 marked the sixtieth anniversary of the liberation of Auschwitz and we must not forget that the evil of Auschwitz was fueled by the illusion of an Aryan ideal—the evil opposite of population thinking.

How often—among ourselves, with our children, neighbors, strangers, and friends—we are tempted to categorize people or urge others to fit some mold of our own making. We try to make them conform to some preconceived notion of who or what or how they should be in order to live up to our expectations. Darwin and liberal religion say that we are individuals, living or trying to live amidst a population.

Darwinism also disabuses us of the illusion that there is anything alive that is unchanging, not a tree, nor a human being, nor any biopopulation—such as a church, for example. "The way leads on," wrote Edwin Muir. "None stays here, none . . . And what will come at last? . . . The way leads on."

Most significantly, evolution by natural selection places enormous responsibility—truly all responsibility—on what we do or don't do with this life. Teleology is a branch of theology concerned with *telos*—that is, end things—that asks, Where are we going? Is it God's purpose that we move toward Armageddon or the Rapture or the progress of humankind onward and upward forever? Darwinism says that all teleology is bunk: we do not know, we cannot know, the story is still being written, revelation is not sealed.

Perhaps most of us are not readers of the *Left Behind* book series, which envisions the end-times salvation of some and the damnation of others. But if that is not our delusion, we are still sometimes deluded by the idea that progressive ideas will ultimately prevail, that superstition and dogma will decline, and, in

the words of Martin Luther King's famous paraphrasing of The-
odore Parker, that "the arc of the moral universe is long, but it
bends toward justice." Darwinism says, No. Nothing is settled in
advance. As Unitarian minister David Rhys Williams said, "We are
the indispensable link between the world that was and the world
that yet shall be. If an arc is to be bent, it is our hands that must
do the bending.

These are not antiseptic observations. The theological issue that
most confronted Charles Darwin's heart was that of justice: If God
is loving and all-powerful, why is there suffering, how can children
die? Married to Emma Wedgewood of the famous pottery-making
Unitarian family, he and Emma were devoted to their eight children. Two died in childhood: their son Charles lived just beyond
his second year; their eldest daughter Annie died of tuberculosis at
ten. Of Annie, Darwin wrote to a friend, "She was my favorite child.
Her cordiality, openness, buoyant joyousness and strong affections
made her most loveable." Twelve years after her death he still spoke
of his "unutterable bitterness" and wept frequently at her loss even
at the end of his life. From my experience as a parish minister,
I know that the loss of a child is simply intolerable.

Darwin was horrified by suffering. He was a generous contrib-
utor to the Society for the Prevention of Cruelty to Animals and he
was outraged when he heard about enslaved and tortured children
in Brazil. Sensitive as he was, he was sometimes literally nauseated
by the reality he articulated in *On the Origin of Species*—that is,
that there is a great procession of life evolving over millions of
years by the blind happenstance of natural selection. He said there
is a "dreadful but quiet war of organic beings . . . in every peaceful
wood and smiling field."

By ethical standards, natural selection is brutal. Over the eons,
whole species have perished and will continue to perish. Millions
upon billions of creatures have suffered and will continue to suffer.
Darwin realized, however, that because nature itself is not sentient
and caring, these realities, however awful, are not ethically unjust.
Were there to be an almighty God who directs this great march of

life—and if God determined to take his beloved daughter Annie from him—that, Darwin concluded, would be the height of injustice and ethically intolerable.

So, because none will do so for us, it becomes our responsibility to behave in ethical ways. According to *Darwin's Religious Odyssey* by William Phipps, Darwin once said to a Dutch student,

> The impossibility of conceiving that this wondrous universe, with our conscious selves, arose through chance, seems to me the chief argument for the existence of God but whether this is an argument of real value, I have never been able to decide. I am aware that if we admit a first cause, the mind still craves to know whence it came, and how it arose. Nor can I overlook the (theological) difficulty (posed by) the immense amount of suffering through the world. I am, also, induced to defer to a certain extent to the judgment of many able people who have fully believed in God; but here again I see how poor an argument this is. The safest conclusion seems to be that the whole subject is beyond the scope of human intellect; but man can do his duty.

It is our responsibility, Darwin said, to preserve love, justice, compassion, forgiveness, and all the other evolved ethical virtues because these are the true expression of our evolved human heart. Evolution does not cause injustice but preserves justice as the noble expression of our humanity.

Unitarian Universalist minister Mark Belletini said in a sermon in 2004,

> Ginko trees don't express a sense of fairness. Human beings do. Perch do not write love sonnets, storks do not express compassion, eels do not wriggle in tenderness when their children laugh. The natural world outside humankind has instinct, and the higher mammals even express elementary

forms of love, but the grand ideas of justice and compassion evolved for the first time with clarity within the human heart.

And so, another of the ways that Darwin and evolution have transformed our culture and informed a liberal understanding of religion is by affirming the priority of justice first, doctrine second. Ortho*praxy*—that is, doing what is right—is so much more vital than having the right opinions, ortho*doxy*. Love comes first; philosophical explanations a distant second.

And what of God? There is an ancient Jewish instruction that, in any given situation, the highest devotion to God is achieved when one acts as if there is no God and acts justly, lovingly, and compassionately nonetheless. The universal acid of Darwinism and evolution by natural selection really do eat through conventional notions of God and we must decide for ourselves whether God is meaningful. William Phipps writes that when a German student inquired about his religious views, Darwin first had a family member respond, "He considers that the theory of Evolution is quite compatible with a belief in a God; but that you must remember that different persons have different definitions of what they mean by God." Yet it is the highly evolved religious imagination of those who conceive of God that assists them in finding their place in this evolving universe. Human beings seem to have brought God into existence, and that existence, for those who believe, is certainly real.

In a 1925 essay, Unitarian minister Jabez Sunderland writes,

Evolution teaches us, as no other thought can do, that the past belongs to us, a heritage infinitely rich and precious. But it belongs to us, not as a stream emptying itself into the present as a pool, to stagnate and dry up and breed disease and die. The past belongs to us as a stream that must flow on through the present into the future, to bless that. If evolution means receiving from what has been, it no less means contributing to what shall be. It means giving. It means making ourselves willingly and joyfully part of God's eternal order. Evolution means a face set to the future, toward which we press with faith and high purpose. It means believing in some better thing, and forever some better thing, for religion, for (humankind), for the world; believing in it so earnestly that we shall gladly make ourselves coworkers with God to bring the consummation.

Love and justice and compassion and forgiveness. Generosity and tolerance and the appreciation of mystery and the unknown. These are part of the legacies of Darwin and Mayr that have touched us and continue to touch us. Respecting that heritage as well as contributing to what shall be, we can affirm their teachings:

Denying that there is any one perfect or unchanging type of any species, we affirm the manifold, imperfect, and unique diversities of life.

Denying that there is anything alive that is unchanging, and knowing that revelation is not sealed, we affirm that we too are an evolving part of the great tide of existence.

Denying that any supernatural power has foreordained our destiny, we affirm that the processes of life are natural processes, that doing and not doctrine matters most, and that we are the ones responsible for bringing our values to fruition—thus making, if you will (and only if you will), God's work truly our own.

Holding Hands with Eve

Gary Kowalski

In a legendary exchange, the year after the publication of Charles Darwin's *On the Origin of Species*, biologist Thomas Henry Huxley met Samuel Wilberforce, the bishop of Oxford, at a gathering of the British Association called to debate the startling new theory that all living beings derived from a common ancestor. The hall was packed. According to one witness, the bishop spoke with a "light, scoffing tone" as he turned a smile on his antagonist and begged to learn, whether it was on his grandmother's or grandfather's side that Mr. Huxley claimed to be descended from an ape? Huxley rose slowly, with dignity, and replied that he was not ashamed to have a monkey for an ancestor—but would be mortified to be associated with a man who used oratorical tricks to obscure the truth.

Were Huxley alive today, he might have responded that his family tree could be traced most easily on his mother's side. While our nuclear DNA comes from both parents, mitochondrial DNA (mtDNA) is strictly matrilineal. It is hard to establish paternal lineage, because nuclear DNA mixes in new combinations with each coupling of sperm and ovum, scrambling each generation. So while I have half my father's genes, I inherited only a quarter of my grandfather's. But the DNA tucked inside intracellular mitochondria never changes. I have exactly the same mtDNA as my mother. And the mtDNA of my wife is precisely the same as that of my daughter and, with slight variations, resembles the mtDNA of every other woman on earth. The variations come from genetic drift—randomly occurring mutations in the genome that take place with statistical regularity over the course of centuries. And because the rate of mutation is relatively constant and predictable over long time spans, a "molecular clock" can be established. This clock tells us that the mtDNA of every woman now living stems from a Mitochondrial Eve who roamed eastern Africa approximately two hundred thousand years ago.

Mitochondrial Eve did not live alone, of course, nor with a mate named Adam. She was in all likelihood the member of a small troop in the vicinity of Kenya, Tanzania, or Ethiopia. Agriculture was far in the future. Hunting and gathering prevailed, organized in groups to take down larger prey. She and others in her band made simple stone tools like hand axes and cleavers. They used fire and tended hearths, passing on their culture as well as their chromosomes to their offspring. While recognizably human, her troop shared the earth and competed with Neanderthals, as well as with now extinct hominids like *Homo erectus* and *Homo heidelbergensis*, whose brain-case was even bigger than our own. Other human species also roamed the world. Diminutive *Homo floresiensis*, about the size of a chimpanzee, evidently had the mental capacity to build boats that reached the Indonesian island of Flores, where the hobbit-sized people died out just twelve thousand years ago. And with these other human-like creatures, Eve shared a common ancestor—another, more distant "Mitochondrial Eve" who lived in the even more remote past.

If we go back far enough, we'd eventually find an Eve common to both animals and homo sapiens. This was the shocking implication of Darwin's theory that so unnerved Bishop Wilberforce—that human beings were not created by the hand of God but evolved through random variation and natural selection. Previously, the immutability of species had been assured. Each living organism was created *sui generis* by an intelligent designer, carefully crafted for its intended niche. For who but a wise and beneficent Providence could have fashioned the marvelous adaptations nature displayed, like the beaks of Galapagos finches—some long and thin for eating insects, some short and stout for cracking seeds, still others perfect for feasting on fruit—each bill wonderfully suited to the precise dietary requirements of its owner? Famously, Darwin suggested that all these variants had arisen from a single progenitor. Migrating from the Pacific coast of South America, the first Galapagos finches found the islands uninhabited by warblers, woodpeckers, or other competitors. Over time, that flock's descendants began to exploit food sources that were previously unavailable. Birds born with a slightly advantageous beak were able to survive in greater numbers and pass on that winning trait. And so, through a process of comparative reproductive success, fourteen separate species eventually arose from the avian pioneers who first colonized the island.

The same process generated every living species, including our own, said Darwin. In *The Descent of Man*, he proposed that human beings were cousins with other primates, a theory that can still shock and enlighten.

To visualize what this means, picture your own mother holding her mother's hand. Now add a link in the chain, so that your grandmother is holding her mother's hand, and another link, so that you have a continuous line of great-grandmothers and now-departed female forebears standing hand in hand (rather like a bucket brigade, passing on ultra-miniature pails of mtDNA). This is your birth line. Imagine this human chain stretching into the distance, farther than the eye can see, so that your matrilineal heritage is an actual, physical line, mapped onto space as well as time. Mitochondrial Eve would be standing somewhere in the line of your foremothers, about ten thousand generations ago, or roughly six miles from the here and now. But she is not at the end of the line, far from it. She had a granny, too.

Now imagine another line of females, facing the one just described. This, too, is a matrilineal succession of daughter, mother, grandmother, and beyond, running parallel to your own. But this second line is a line of chimpanzees, our closest relative. For miles (and years), the two lines would seemingly run like train tracks, never approaching each other. And this appearance—that each creature invariably gives rise to its own kind, never deviating from its own genotype—accounts for the pre-Darwinian confidence in the immutability of species. But if you followed the two lines reaching into the distance, you would notice them slowly beginning to converge, the chimpanzees standing slightly closer to their human counterparts. And finally, at a point located about 160 miles away—roughly 5 million years ago—you would discover a single figure, standing in the middle of the track, so to speak. Her right hand grasps the hand of her daughter in the human line, the genus *Homo*. Her left hand joins the hand of her other daughter, in the genus *Pan*, the lineage that includes modern chimps and bonobos. This is the primordial mother, animal and human, who gave birth to us all—not just a hypothetical figure, but an actual individual.

The fossil record and the molecular clock tell us when she lived. Chimpanzees share most of the genetic code that makes us human. One recent study from the Chimp Sequencing and Analysis Consortium, reported in *Nature*, found a 96-percent match between the two species, while another team working at the Wayne State University School of Medicine put the correlation at 99.4 percent. The differences in the findings depend on which pieces of the sequence you measure and consider important. These discrepancies skew the date of our human genesis; perhaps our two lines diverged 7 million years ago, rather than only 5. But the 1 to 4 percent that distinguishes chimp from human is small compared to our joint genetic inheritance, and minor compared to the 40 percent that separates us from rats and mice. It means that human beings and apes are not only kin biologically but related emotionally and psychologically as well.

Our appreciation of what we have in common has grown in the last fifty years. For instance, like us, chimpanzees are cultural animals. Some wild bands (but not all) have learned to swing rocks to crack heavy-shelled panda nuts. Calibrating the force is difficult. Up to a ton of pressure may be needed to split the husk and reach the nutritious kernel, but pounding too hard smashes the nut and renders it inedible. Chimps have been observed carefully collecting proper pounding stones, flat-faced on one side but easy to grasp on the other, to use and pass on to the next generation, in what resembles a family tradition.

In the wild, chimps use a variety of vocalizations to communicate, while in more controlled settings, bonobos like Kanzi and his sister Panbanisha, who reside at the Great Ape Trust in Iowa, have mastered hundreds of lexigrams and understand complex spoken English. Wearing a welder's mask to prevent non-verbal cues, Kanzi's trainer Susan Savage-Rumbaugh asks Kanzi to put pine needles in the refrigerator and carry out other unlikely tasks, receiving perfect compliance each time. On an outing in the woods, Kanzi touches the symbols for "marshmallows" and "fire." Given a handful of twigs, he snaps them, kindles them with a match, and toasts marshmallows on a stick. As well as "making fire," Kanzi has learned to craft Oldowan-style cutting knives like those found by paleontologists Louis and Mary Leakey in the Olduvai Gorge where humans originated. The tools are crude but easily cut hide and rope.

None of this was known a half century ago. When Jane Goodall first ventured to Africa in 1960, no long-term field studies of the chimpanzee existed. She and her students were the first to understand that chimpanzees organize themselves into bands that cooperate in hunting and sharing food (rather like the troop of Mitochondrial Eve). She introduced us to the apes' gentle side, their hugging, kissing, snuggling, and long playful childhoods so like our own. When Goodall first observed the chimpanzees selecting wands of grass to fish for termites, the discovery so rocked the scientific community that her mentor, Louis Leakey, suggested it might be time to redefine the meaning of "tool," redefine "human," or simply admit that chimpanzees were people, too.

That last suggestion finds support among biologists, who have begun to group all the Great Apes (including gorillas, orangutans, and chimps, along with you and me) into the same taxonomic family, *hominidae*, previously reserved for human beings. Some would go farther. Writing in the *Proceedings of the National Academy of Sciences*, Dr. Derek Wildman, head of the Wayne State team that found the closest genetic correlation between people and chimps, suggests that chimpanzees and bonobos be reclassified as members of our own genus, *Homo*.

The repercussions would reach far beyond the specialization of primatologists, challenging the privileged place human beings assign themselves in nature. Because for Bishop Wilberforce, and most moralists and theologians to this day, the offspring who traced their descent from their grandmother's left hand—the chimpanzees and bonobos—were an entirely different order from those who traced their ancestry to her right hand. Those in one line possessed an immortal soul, while those in the other had none. Those in one line were rational free agents; those in the other were driven by brute instinct. Standing in the human line entitled you to legal protections, including the right to own, buy, and sell property, while standing in the animal line meant you were a commodity that could be traded and exchanged. Those on the grandmother's right hand had biographies, while those on her left merely had biologies—they were less active subjects with their own preferences and desires than they were passive objects to be used as resources, as the book of Genesis commanded. Human beings had dominion, in fact and by right. So the worst insult the bishop could hurl (causing at least one Victorian lady to faint dead away) was to compare the esteemed Mr. Huxley's grandmother to a knuckle-walker. The divide between children of the biblical mother Eve and other living creatures was absolute.

But Charles Darwin erased the hard boundary separating human beings from other living creatures. In his 1872 publication, *The Expression of Emotions in Animals and Man*, he compared some of the special affinities of people and other primates, finding the latter's capacities for joy and sorrow "closely analogous to those of man." If a young chimpanzee is tickled (and he noted that "the armpits are sensitive to tickling, as in the case of our children"), a chuckling or laughing sound is uttered, with the corners of the mouth drawn back and lower eyelids wrinkled, like our own. "Young Orangs, when tickled, likewise grin and make a chuckling sound; and Mr. Martin says that their eyes grow brighter. As soon as their laughter ceases, an expression may be detected passing over their faces, which, as Mr. Wallace remarked to me, may be called a smile." At the same time, "the appearance of dejection in young orangs and chimpanzees, when out of health, is as plain and almost as pathetic as in the case of our children. This state of mind and body is shown by their listless movements, fallen countenances, dull eyes, and changed complexion." He includes several accounts of monkeys in grief actually shedding tears. Any objective observer, Darwin concludes, "will be forced to admit that the movements of their features and their gestures are almost as expressive as those of man."

Apes may share mental and emotional states similar to our own, but are they also aware of their feelings? Perhaps anger and delight slip through their minds with no lasting sense of a "self" who experiences these pangs. Self-consciousness in human infants is usually tested by mirror recognition. Between the age of two and three, babies begin to identify their own reflections in a looking glass, making the crucial distinction between "self" and "other" and establishing a stable sense of personal identity. Although psychologists hadn't invented the mirror recognition test at that point, Darwin shares the following anecdote:

> Many years ago, in the Zoological Gardens, I placed a looking-glass on the floor before two young orangs, who, as far as it was known, had never before seen one. At first they gazed at their own images with the most steady surprise, and often changed their point of view. They then approached close and protruded their lips towards the image, as if to kiss it, in exactly the same manner as they had previously done towards each other, when first placed, a few days before, in the same room. They next made all

sorts of grimaces, and put themselves in various attitudes before the mirror; they pressed and rubbed the surface; they placed their hands at different distances behind it; looked behind it; and finally seemed almost frightened, started a little, became cross, and refused to look any longer.

The orangutans were puzzled, but probably not fooled. For now we know that all Great Apes (along with a variety of other creatures, including orcas, bottle-nosed dolphins, elephants, and some birds) pass the litmus test. Surreptitiously put a dab of rouge on Kanzi's forehead and put him before a mirror. His hand immediately reaches, not toward the reflected image, but for his own brow to investigate the curious crimson mark. While vanity is supposedly a human failing, most chimps (like most teenagers) will happily spend hours in front of the mirror, brushing their teeth, making faces, and contemplating their own appearance.

All of this forces us to look into the mirror also, and do some hard self-examination. If chimpanzees belong to the genus *Homo*, based on their anatomy and cognitive ability, does that mean they deserve human rights? Should primates be used in biomedical research, or kept in zoos? Used for crash dummies? Hunted for sport or bushmeat? Britain and New Zealand have long banned using chimps in the lab. Spain recently became the first nation granting legal rights to apes, stipulating that they cannot be tortured or exhibited in circuses. Other countries are likely to follow suit. Once the biological line separating human from animal has been crossed, ethical and legal boundaries also have to be redrawn.

Darwin himself struggled with the moral implications of his theory. A lifelong animal lover who surrounded himself with dogs and other pets (Darwin's turtle died only recently, at the age of 176), he was aghast at any form of cruelty or abuse. As an angler, he regularly dipped his worms in brine before impaling them on the hook, to render the little creatures senseless. His son relates how the great biologist returned from his afternoon walk one day shaken and pale from encountering a draughtsman mistreating his horse, agitated from having remonstrated with the man. The thought of any creature in pain was almost unbearable, and in a letter to Professor Ray Lancaster, he confessed that the practice of experimentation on living beings made him "sick with horror." Darwin mused, "Every one has heard of the dog suffering under vivisection, who licked the hand of the operator; this man, unless the operation was fully justified by an increase of our knowledge, or unless he had a heart of stone, must have felt remorse to the last hour of his life." While animal research might be a terrible necessity in some circumstances, he felt it should never be pursued for "mere damnable and detestable curiosity." His own work laid the cornerstone for modern biology, but required no lab animals. With a better understanding than most of how closely we are all related, the great scientist was also a great humanitarian.

Two hundred years after Darwin's birth, the time has arrived to complete the revolution he started, by understanding that other living creatures are members of our moral community—sensitive social beings like ourselves—as well as our biological kin. While linking hands with our own parents and progeny we must also reach across the species barrier to join hands in sympathy with the animals who are our partners in everything that matters most.

New research shows that monkeys even possess a sense of fairness. Train two female capuchins to perform a similar task, but reward the first with a bland slice of cucumber and the second with a tasty grape. When she sees the inequity, the first monkey will refuse to cooperate with the game, which offends her idea of right and wrong. How, then, do we justify the notion of human supremacy, or the claim that the fruits of justice belong exclusively to the sons and daughters of Adam and Eve?

Even apes, we know, can reach beyond the species line, like Binti Jua of Chicago's Brookfield Zoo. When a toddler inadvertently tumbled into the gorilla's enclosure, knocking himself unconscious, the female silverback (with her own eighteen-month-old baby clinging to her fur) approached the young child to protect him from the more aggressive males nearby. Then Binti carried the boy to the exit door, waiting with him until staff and paramedics could arrive. Why should we be surprised? Binti (whose name in Swahili means "Daughter of Sunlight") was helping a fellow primate, another member of the *hominidae* family, with whom she shared a common capacity for nurturing and love.

Gorilla, chimp, orangutan, and human—we are all the children of a single mother. We are all holding hands with Eve.

An Imperfect Legacy

Naomi King

While there are many spiritual lessons to be found in Charles Darwin's work and life, one of the greatest and most challenging for us today arises from his struggle with infamy and his yearning for approval. His most lastingly controversial work is not *On the Origin of Species* (1859) but *The Descent of Man* (1871)—a text that was remarkably noncontroversial when it was published. In *The Descent of Man*, Darwin succumbs to speculation, applies his previous work to the social orders, and establishes the basis for what will become known as "social Darwinism." While he furthers the case laid out by his fellow biologist Thomas Henry Huxley in *Man's Place in Nature,* the story of humanity that Darwin portrays becomes a justification for Victorian British Imperial policy: The most evolved human is the white man and the other races descend in degrees of darkness toward our ape-like ancestors. The nuance offered initially by Darwin and defended by Huxley, that all of humanity has a common ancestor, was lost to the culture in which Darwin and Huxley lived. *The Descent of Man* spurred the unfortunate history of racism and bigotry forward with a purportedly scientific edge. The book captivated and influenced religious liberals and became the core of eugenicist literature such as educator David Starr Jordan's *Blood of a Nation.*

Written over a decade after *On the Origin of Species, The Descent of Man* was composed by a Darwin who had grown both more infirm and isolated and more accustomed to adulation, fame, and respect. His place in Victorian society as a gentleman scientist—which permitted him to publish his theory of evolution prior to fellow naturalist Alfred Russel Wallace—became more fully entrenched in the establishment as he aged. While *Origin* in many ways boldly launches some important claims, it became accepted by John Stuart Mill and other intellectuals precisely because it echoed the already accepted theories of Thomas Malthus, Jean-Baptiste Lamarck, and Herbert Spencer. In *Origin* Darwin was circumspect about religious beliefs and matters, but nearly twenty years later he had changed his tone, and only due to his publisher's squirming did he make some attempts to moderate the language in *Descent* to a more broadly popular religious sensibility. Unlike when he published *Origin*, Darwin was no longer unsure of himself, though he was still anxious about public abuse.

The Descent of Man reflects the values of Victorian society. Darwin asserts that the Golden Rule—"Do unto others as you would have others do unto you"—evolved as the basis of morality in a form of spiritual selection. A society not based on the Golden Rule would be a failed one, doomed to extinction. Darwin takes on the voice of the biblical prophets, but with a Malthusian twist. Instead of preaching radical equality amongst humanity in evolution, he accepts social practice and national institutions as evidence of evolution in action. He writes,

> The remarkable success of the English as colonists over other European nations . . . has been ascribed to their "daring and persistent energy;" but who can say how the English gained their energy? There is apparently much truth in the belief that the wonderful progress of the United States, as well as the character of the people, are the results of natural selection; the more energetic, restless, and courageous men from all parts of Europe having emigrated during the last ten or twelve generations.

In *Origin,* Darwin justifies social norms as evolution in action—revealed in key Malthusian concepts such as "competition, struggle, adaptation, success, and extinction." But since he is dependent upon the emerging study of ethnology for so much of his material, Darwin offers the world a philosophical treatise in the guise of a scientific text.

Descent famously includes support for naturalist Pierre Paul Broca's work asserting that skull size correlates to intelligence in human beings, but not between species. Darwin chooses to support Broca's work rather than Louis Pierre Gratiolet's challenges (which were supported by Huxley's own research, yet Huxley, too, drew on Broca's ethnology), because they result in less social disruption and legitimize European conquest and domination of other human societies. Any whiff of egalitarianism undermined science of the era, and any scientist who promoted egalitarianism lost the respect of his peers. Huxley himself encountered strong social pressure when he was accused of egalitarianism just for selling *Man's Place in Nature* at railway station newspaper stalls— even though it was not a book promoting social equality. Darwin wondered that Huxley had not been aware of how improper it was for gentleman's science—*real* science—to be sold and taught to the masses. Another way Darwin responded to social pressure was how he accepted and trusted the information he received from socially respectable observers, while laboriously duplicating and checking the work of his less respectable sources—the pigeon and poultry breeders, keepers of hounds, and other men of the lower classes who served as his devoted informants. Broca belonged to the class of scientists with which one could quibble, but Darwin didn't need to do so, since he supported evolution. However, unlike Broca, Darwin believed that evolution could be random and not necessarily linear. But when it came to social evolution in human beings, Darwin did advocate linear evolution and hierarchies. He supported the social order in which he lived, defended his friends' previous work, and was less controversial to the theological liberals who supported him.

Darwin recapitulates the ethnology of Broca and fellow French naturalist Georges Cuvier, mixing in Mill and Malthus, describing human evolution from barbarism to civilization, defending a moral and spiritual selection no longer dependent upon the biblical account of creation. One of the arguments against both higher biblical criticism and the theory of evolution is that they destabilize the social order and strip away the basis for moral practice. If there is no God-given order, then what is there? Darwin contends that there is a logical hierarchy that reflects the lives of those in power, even if it calls into question the accounts of human creation in Genesis. The spiritual selection of the dominant world power of the time represents evolution in action.

Darwin was concerned about the weakening of his society because of what he thought of as its highly evolved morality. The Victorian world was replete with societies to care for those viewed as weaker and unable to care for themselves in a competitive and brutal world. Darwin acknowledged, therefore, that the weak would continue to have children, and pass on their weaknesses. He saw marital reform as a necessary social check to prevent social weakness from allowing another nation to evolve ahead of his own.

> The surgeon may harden himself while performing an operation, for he knows that he is acting for the good of his patient; but if we were intentionally to neglect the weak and helpless, it could only be for a contingent benefit, with a certain and great present evil. Hence we must bear without complaining the undoubtedly bad effects of the weak surviving and propagating their kind; but there appears to be at least one check in steady action, namely the weaker and inferior members of society not marrying so freely as the sound; and this check might be indefinitely increased, though this is more to be hoped for than expected, by the weak in body or mind refraining from marriage.

George Darwin, Charles's son, promoted social reform in an 1873 *Contemporary Review* article, arguing for governmental permission to allow divorce and contraception to help curb undesirable behaviors that weakened British society. The implications of Darwin's work were obvious to his children and to the world—his work justifies social engineering through eugenics. Social engineering would ensure that some countries would remain the way they thought they had become through evolution—as spiritually and intellectually superior.

Darwin was not unaware of the implications of his arguments. He was also not unaware that it felt good to feel superior and applauded and right.

> But there is another and much more powerful stimulus to the development of the social virtues, namely, the praise and blame of our fellow-men. The love of approbation and the dread of infamy, as well as the bestowal of praise or blame, are primarily due, as we have seen in the third chapter, to the instinct of sympathy; and this instinct no doubt was originally acquired, like all the other social instincts, through natural selection.

We who live in an age that has returned to the question of the social emotions, to affective neuroscience using contemporary tools for understanding the social framework, can agree with Darwin that affective states are indeed acquired through natural selection, while being nurtured and refined by social connections. But we would also do well to remember the difficulty in moving outside of our own acceptable meaning-making systems. When Darwin first moved outside of his own, it took him decades to write his conclusions down. Part of what allowed him to record those conclusions is that they had started to become more accepted in his social milieu. Thomas Malthus and Paul Broca had joined Darwin in promoting these ideas of competition and linear progression. While *Origin* may have become the rallying

point for a new world view, *Descent*, for the most part, recapitu-
lated the status quo.

Contemporary religious liberals who affirm and claim Darwin
often speak of a spiritual selection. We can assert truth without
superstition—or so we like to say—inferring that religious liberalism is an evolved religion, more evolved than other religious view-
points. The spiritual selection we speak of is not formally endorsed;
officially, we are egalitarians. But I rarely visit liberal congregations where someone does not burst forth with pride in observing,
"We're the smart ones," or "Ours is the evolved religion."

Religions, like other social systems, change over time. Con-
flicts between religious systems are often about different understandings of what is morally superior. But in affirming spiritual
selection, we trod a road already worn by Darwin. Choosing spiritual selection violates liberal religious principles of equity and
human rights that emerged in response to the great horrors of
social engineering that were justified by *The Descent of Man* and
made real in the twentieth century. We need to learn the lessons of
humility and common connection more completely, integrating
them into our personal meaning-making systems in order for us
to create the egalitarian world we espouse. Let us heed Darwin's
cautionary tale. We laud and lift up Darwin, but like all of us, he
had his foibles and failings, and many of these are revealed for all
to see in *The Descent of Man*. Fortunately, I prefer my anointed
heroes to be human, with all their foibles, for that allows me to
learn and gives me hope. Darwin was not more evolved than me,
and I am not more evolved than him. We live in different ages and
arise from different experiences. I come after the Shoah and the
great eugenicist movement in the United States and continue to
live in a time of genocides. I empathize with the disempowered
in those situations. But that was not Darwin's experience, worldview, or empathy.

I find five lessons we can learn from Charles Darwin's life and
experiences. These are five spiritual practices for those of us who
inherit or claim his spiritual ancestry.

First, like Darwin, we can excel in paying attention to tiny details. *Origin* was followed by an exquisite text, *Fertilisation of Orchids* (1862), which required Darwin to continue his focused detailed observations on sexual selection as the means of natural selection. The details are absorbing in themselves, and filled with transporting wonder—as Darwin's family and friends frequently observed of him lost in reverie of the worlds of the minute and spectacular.

Secondly, when we are caught up in the wonder and mystery of the moment, moment after moment, we can use this multitude of experiences to form our own patterning principles. We can stay true to a principle of religious liberalism that names the shaping value of direct experience of that transcendent mystery and wonder. We can ensure that we don't move out too swiftly on the tides of popularity, rather than on experience and observation, yet we can also play with our imaginations in generating larger patterns from these little details.

Thirdly, when we edit our observations into a coherent consistent whole through the use of reason and wonder, we exploit our evolved capacity for story and may, like Darwin, tell a new and compelling piece of that story.

Fourthly, we need to stay in relationship with an esteemed community while looking beyond the boundaries of that community to those who are not esteemed or in the center of it. Darwin corresponded with all kinds of informants, so that his world was not entirely limited to his immediate surroundings. Yet his reliance on the support of his circle of friends, such as the X Club, contributed to the development of *The Descent of Man*. A self-reinforcing circular society may pass for peer review and a broad world, but the very comfort of it can alert us that we may need to seek some new perspectives and energy. That doesn't mean breaking with our community, but it does mean expanding who's in our community.

Fifthly, Darwin's example teaches that we can be and do great things and still make terrible mistakes that can have horrific consequences. I cannot imagine a more hopeful or important lesson for our current social milieu, driven by the twenty-four-hour news cycle, which feasts on human flaws and destroys people's lives. Picking and choosing parts of Darwin and his life is not really possible; *Origin* is full of what he develops in *Descent*. But we can take heart in knowing the legacies we inherit from him, and applying ourselves to the work of accepting ourselves and one another as always unfinished, imperfect beings on this endless spiritual journey of learning.

Like all of us, Darwin had his struggles. He proved again his assertion that we are indeed social animals when he succumbed to the temptation to mix natural philosophy, moral philosophy, and moral economy. By relying on Herbert Spencer, John Stuart Mills, and Thomas Malthus, he ended up closer to Jean-Baptiste Larmarck and Louis Agassis than he—and we, his contemporary spiritual inheritors—might have otherwise wished. The intertwining of moral and natural philosophy into one hawser anchors our spiritual tradition. But the way it is so spliced and knotted and slung around in all kinds of wretched conditions and purposes, that hawser has also become, as it was with Darwin, one of our greatest weaknesses. We are, as he was, creatures of our culture. We yearn for esteem, girded with the grandest tokens that our society affords. What appears to be scientific proof of our claims also seems to be supported by and to support the health of the economy—this is the ideology of spiritual selection. The work that lies before us is to pick up where this spiritual forebear could no longer go, and develop further, selecting for ourselves a direction of greater equity, compassion, connection, and love.

We Are Stardust

Connie Barlow

The epic of evolution is a grand narrative that pertains to everyone, everywhere in the world. It is the story of creation drawn from the worldwide, self-correcting enterprise of scientific discovery. Charles Darwin pioneered our modern understanding of the long developmental history of life on earth, just as James Hutton and Charles Lyell had earlier established that even the tallest of mountains rise and erode, rise and erode. By the middle of the twentieth century, scientists had discovered that even the heavens are not immortal—and thank goodness that this is so. Previous generations of stars that lived and explosively died before our sun was born created all the complex atoms that now reside in and around us. Now even the vast cosmos is perceived as not only ancient, but evolving—creatively evolving.

A grand narrative that pertains to everyone—and that we would teach our children wholeheartedly—may seem contrary to the identity politics and religious tolerance championed by religious liberals. But to remain on the vanguard of progressive values, it is time for religious liberals to place our celebration of diversity within a wider arc that offers the promise of universal relevance and a sense of global community. Ecotheologian Thomas Berry calls this sacred evolutionary worldview a *metareligious* perspective.

Astrophysicist Joel Primack and cultural historian Nancy Ellen Abrams also call for this unified outlook. In their 2006 book, *The*

View from the Center of the Universe, they write,

> Without a meaningful, *believable* story that explains the world we actually live in, people have no idea how to think about the big picture. And without a big picture, we are very small people. A human without a cosmology is like a pebble lying near the top of a great mountain, in contact with its little indentation in the dirt and pebbles immediately surrounding it, but oblivious to its stupendous view.

And the educational innovator Maria Montessori writes this in her 1948 book, *To Educate the Human Potential*,

> Educationalists in general agree that imagination is important, but they would have it cultivated as separate from intelligence, just as they would separate the latter from the activity of the hand. . . . In the school they want children to learn dry facts of reality, while their imagination is cultivated by fairy tales, concerned with a world that is certainly full of marvels, but not the world around them in which they live. On the other hand, by offering the child the story of the universe, we give him something a thousand times more infinite and mysterious to reconstruct with his imagination, a drama no fable can reveal.

There is no creation story anywhere in the world that can exceed the wonder of an epic tale that teaches that we, in truth, are made of stardust. No story of transformation can offer a closer kinship with all life than the epic adventure of a fish hauling out onto land and becoming amphibian, of a reptile taking to the air and becoming bird, of a mammal slipping back into the sea and becoming whale, of a primate climbing down from a tree and becoming us.

Several years ago, while guest teaching a religious education class for young teens, I decided to test a hunch. "Tell me some creation stories from around the world," I challenged. Hands shot up and I heard about the Garden of Eden and about the classical Greek myths and one Native American story.

"Good," I congratulated them. "Now, tell me: What's *your* creation story?" Silence. No hands went up. So I walked over to one side of the room and began to walk out a timeline across the floor. I said, "In the beginning, what scientists call the big bang, what we like to call the great radiance, all that came out of the fireball were the simplest atoms: gases of hydrogen and helium."

"Oh," one of the boys spoke up, "that's what we're learning in science class!" Yes, that's what they are learning in science class—if they are lucky. As liberals know all too well, the teaching of cosmic evolution, chemical evolution, geological evolution, human evolution, and biological evolution is not offered in many public schools in America. That deficiency will surely continue. Until the majority of churches in America preach evolution enthusiastically at the pulpit and teach it in inspiring ways, we will never see an end to the war between science and religion in America. If liberal religious people don't have the courage to teach the grand evolutionary story in our own religious communities—and not just as one option, but as humanity's best collective understanding of history and reality—then who will?

The children I taught that day in Florida were surprised to hear that what they were learning in science class—and on the Discovery Channel and Animal Planet—might have something to do with religion. They were surprised to learn that they, too, could have a creation story and that it needn't include any beliefs contrary to the discoveries of science. Until that moment, their world had been fragmented—there was religion and there was science. There was fact and there was belief. The two realms had never been tied together. Joseph Campbell, in his *Power of Myth* television series with Bill Moyers, defined religion in this simple and practical way: Religion is "that which puts one in accord with the universe." So if religious liberals do not make a priority of guiding our children and youth into an intimate, empowering relationship with the universe, we fail to provide them with religion. The root *religio* means to yoke together—to yoke all of one's learnings and experiences into a coherent, life-giving worldview.

We should also do our best to provide the next generations with a healthy sense of what being religious or spiritual actually means—and does not mean. Otherwise, religious questions and challenges from friends who attend conservative churches will lead our young people to conclude that their status as religious people is determined by the substance of their beliefs. *Spirituality* can be defined as right relationship with reality at all levels—the inner and the outer, the social and the ecological, the past and the future. Right relationship means not just how we act but how we feel in each of those relationships. Do we feel gratitude, trust? Do we feel at ease, authentic? Will our ways of relating to reality carry us through times of sorrow and suffering? Do they inspire us to be all we can be? Only right relationship at all levels of reality will give us a chance to achieve the practical outcomes of effective religious orientations—personal wholeness, social coherence, and ecological integrity.

Yes, religious liberals can teach our children that evolution is our creation story. While adults may benefit from reflecting on the Greek myths, or Native American creation tales, or the Genesis accounts read as poetry, children do not live in a world of metaphor and abstraction. Due to their developmental level, elementary age children find the nuances of reality difficult to understand. If we don't give them solid answers to their big questions, you can bet that the children they meet on the playground who go to other churches certainly will.

Later, when our children enter middle school and in the years beyond, we can encourage them to question. They can second guess everything we have taught them, everything they have heard from their peers and culture, and come up with their own responses to the mysteries of life and the cosmos.

A religious educator at a Unitarian Universalist congregation once used a curriculum that each week presented a different creation story from around the world. She had difficulty because several children invariably broke into the storytelling saying, "That's not the way it happened!" or "That's not true!" The protests only ceased during the final session—which presented the origin story drawn from modern science.

Several years ago a colleague showed me the "coming of age" statement written by her teenage son as part of his liberal church's religious exploration program. After studying various faith traditions and considering fundamental life questions, the youth had written that he really didn't have a belief one way or the other about what, if anything, happens to the soul after death. Indeed, his entire speech centered on what he didn't know and what he didn't believe. For a sixteen-year-old with precious little life experience, such a stance not only makes sense, it is commendable. Yet the boy concluded his recitation by characterizing himself as "not really spiritual."

Religious advisors and mentors had failed this boy. Beliefs, particularly about supernatural claims, are not, after all, the core of what religion means in liberal religious circles. What counts are religio-spiritual states of mind and action—notably, gratitude, forgiveness, compassion, communion with something greater than oneself, commitment to a cause, service, and trust in the larger realms of existence. Had the boy experienced any of these aspects of spirituality? Did he know that a deliberate refusal to adopt a creedal statement of faith was something that not only applied to his religious heritage but could also apply to himself? After all, religious liberals and seekers as a group insist that we be counted among the faithful. Yet those who likewise shirk a creedal statement may be no less religious than those who claim allegiance to a creed of their own making.

At the home of a religious education director, I leafed through a new curriculum developed for teens that included a session on death. It encouraged teens to reflect on what that concept means to them. For background, they were to watch the 1990 movie *Ghost* and then discuss it. The male lead character is murdered but remains a voyeur in this world until he can ensure that justice is done and his girlfriend is safe. In this way, the teens are led into discussing the ineffable—do ghosts really exist, and does one's spirit live on in some way after death? So the emphasis is on belief or disbelief, not in cultivating right relationship with the inevitability of death—of one's own death and the deaths of loved ones.

In contrast, the evolutionary sciences offer religious liberals substantial tools for helping our children and youth develop healthy and life-giving perspectives on death. Understanding our evolutionary origins and the vital, creative role that death plays in cosmic chemistry, the creation of continents, the complexification of life, and ecological sustainability provides a comforting and crucial perspective that we can offer younger generations—and ourselves. Indeed, for the first four years of my husband's and my itinerant evolutionary ministry, the program I usually presented as guest educator in classrooms and as the theme for intergenerational services was "We Are Made of Stardust!" Teaching kids in fun and memorable ways that the very atoms of their bodies were fashioned inside ancestor stars who lived and died before our own star, the sun, was born is deeply satisfying work. It helps children develop life-giving attitudes about death.

Religious conservatives who base their theology on a literal reading of the Bible have a ready explanation for why pets and people, including loved ones, have to die. Conservative Christians look to several passages from the writings of Paul as the definitive interpretation of the fall from grace. Romans 5:12 reads, "Wherefore as by one man sin entered this world, and by sin death, so death passed upon all men." So because Adam disobeyed God and ate fruit from the forbidden tree, God punished not only the first humans but all the generations to come, as well as all the other species on Earth. God did this by bringing death into the world. Paul understood the mythic story to mean that there was no death in the garden initially—not by old age, nor even in the course of ecological interactions. There were no carnivores or scavengers in those days, no diseases, no unfortunate accidents. Even T. Rex was a vegetarian—until the fall.

But liberals freeze when our four-year-old one day calmly asks us the big question about death. How do we respond? Sadly, for many of us the inauthenticity or discomfort we convey in our response overrides whatever the actual content may be. Our kids sense that this is a taboo subject, something really scary. Yet it need not be so.

In addition to guiding children toward a felt relationship with the heavens, an embodied communion with the stars, and pride in their stellar ancestry, we can offer a "cosmic container" for understanding death in natural, yet comforting, ways. This container must be robust enough to safely carry them through their own times of sorrow and encourage them to fully feel and express grief. Children should know in their bones that death plays a creative role in the cosmos. Without the death of stars and the explosive recycling of complex atoms that stars squeeze into existence during their bright lives, there would be no planets or life today. The primordial clouds of gas that continue to birth new stars must contain something more than simple hydrogen and helium in order for planets to form. They must also harbor atoms of carbon, calcium, nitrogen, potassium, and many more. In essence, star-birthing regions of the galaxy must be seeded with stardust, the gift of previous generations of stars, in order for rocky planets to form. Similarly, without the death of pets and people, there would soon be no room for any more puppies and babies to be born. The circle of life depends on death. It is natural and necessary. Death will come to all of us.

This naturalized, sacralized understanding of death should be introduced to our children at a very early age, with continuing opportunities for deepening and personalizing their understanding and for learning more of the wondrous, reassuring science that supports such a view. Questions about what happens to the spirit of the pet or the person or the squashed possum along the road may be answered in a variety of ways, tempered to the family's inclinations. Or, as religious educator Sophia Fahs advocated, we can invite the child to imagine for herself. But the basic appreciation of the fact of death, and that it comes to all of us—though in some cases too early and in ways that may make us very sad—is absolutely vital in liberal religious settings.

I once spent an evening with elementary-age children at a large Unitarian Universalist church in New Jersey, teaching the science and meaning of stardust. After talking about the gifts created by our ancestor stars, I asked the children, "Do any of you have a grandparent who has already become an ancestor?" Instead of hesitancy, the children proudly raised their hands. One boy said, "My grandma became an ancestor on January 26, 2004." A year later I took my stardust program to a children's group at a small church in Mississippi. I concluded that session by having us all sit in a circle on the floor and chant a song about stardust while glittering one another to symbolize that we truly are made of stardust. Still sitting in the circle, I asked, "Did any of you learn something here that you didn't know before and that you think you will remember for the rest of your life?" An eight-year-old girl who had come to church with her grandmother responded, "I learned that my grandmother will die."

What an honor—and a responsibility—to bring this science-based understanding of death to even our youngest children in sacred ways and in sacred contexts. Religious liberals no longer need to feel uncomfortable or disingenuous when answering children's questions about death. Our very own cosmic creation story—*their* cosmic creation story—has strong and comforting answers about why death is in the world and how everything we love in this universe in some way depends on death. Questions about what happens to soul, spirit, and consciousness after death will still call forth a variety of responses from parents and the children themselves. But as religious educators, we can nurture healthy understandings of death that provide a universal, science-based foundation that transcends the supernatural/natural divide.

One of my favorite anecdotes from my traveling ministry comes from an email I received from a young mother. I had presented a five-minute children's story on stardust at her church. She wrote:

> My children are six and eight and I have been floundering with how to raise them spiritually. I liked the idea of

exposing them to all the stories, to teaching them that different people and different cultures have different pathways to the same thing: that great mystery. The Unitarian Universalist church is a good fit for that, but something was missing: a story of their own. And now they have one and they both really get it!

My daughter said to me as I was tucking her into bed the other night, "Mom, did you know our sun will die in about 5 billion years? That's kind of sad." Just as I was searching for something to say, she continued in a very hopeful tone, "Maybe I'll see it! Maybe I'll be an animal like a deer by then, because it probably takes a really long time to become an animal."

Thank you for teaching my children that they are stardust, for giving them a story, and for being there at just the right time for me.

At an ecospirituality conference in Lexington, Kentucky, I ended my plenary talk on stardust by quoting Carl Sagan. Sagan had concluded his 1980 television series *Cosmos* with these words: "We are the local embodiment of a cosmos grown to self-awareness. We have begun to contemplate our origins: starstuff pondering the stars!"

Immediately after the talk, a young woman approached me, tears in her eyes. She said, "I was seven years old when *Cosmos* aired, and it changed my life." "How?" I asked with amazement. "I learned I was related to everything!"

Relationship, a sense of belonging, feeling at home in the universe—the epic of evolution is ideal for fulfilling these basic human needs. My husband, Michael Dowd, once received an email from a young woman after a talk he gave at a church. It said, "Whenever I read about us being stardust, I feel, even if only for a fleeting moment, limitless. I may only be nineteen, but no other religion, philosophy, or theory I have encountered has ever been able to do that."

Edward O. Wilson, the world's most respected living evolutionist and the 1999 "Humanist of the Year," asserts that religion is central to culture. But God is not central to religion. The God question, while marginal to evolutionists seeking natural explanations for the power and persistence of religion, is no marginal issue when teaching our children. This is the case even in humanist-leaning congregations and families because children pick up on popular culture, which equates religion with beliefs in and about God. In addition, children naturally pass through a "magical-mythic" phase. They will create their own enchanting explanations whether or not we provide them with heirloom fables and miracle stories—or with enchantingly told renditions of the science story.

Parents sense that grown-up perspectives may be beyond the reach of children. So even when a child pointedly demands, "But what do *you* believe about God, Daddy?" we are careful to convey our own truths in ways that will not cause unnecessary trouble for our offspring out on the playground. Recall the "heresy" that distinguishes liberal religion: there is no fiery hell. A loving God would not be so cruel, even to the worst offenders. Everyone, universally, is "saved." So when a child is asked by her friend, "Are you saved?" we can advise her to answer simply (and truthfully), "Yes."

Michael Dowd advises that before assessing the truth value of any claim we should notice whether its spoken or written expression puts it in the realm of "day language" or "night language." Day language pertains to objective, measurable truth—the facts as they really are, and as best we understand them. Crucially, day language is supplemented with a genuine "We just don't know" for any glaring gaps in our grasp of objective reality.

In contrast, night language is dreamlike, inspired metaphor that gives voice and meaning to real human experiences that lack, or once lacked, objective causal explanations. Without having to present a child with a dissertation on the distinction between day and night language, a religiously liberal parent might draw from both categories when answering any of these questions: "Is there a God?" "Who is God?" "Will God take care of me?" "Where does

God live?" "Do you ever talk to God?" or "Can God see me?"

Notice the possibilities offered in this sample explanation: The word *God* means a lot of different things to different people. If what you mean by God is kind of like a father or a mother somewhere up in the sky or out in space—someone who cares about you in the way that I care about you, then, no, there is no God. But if what you mean by God is more about awesome things—like the fact that it took the entire universe almost fourteen billion years to make this moment in your life possible, or that there is a bright warm sun up in the sky that we can absolutely depend on, or that you are surrounded by people who love you very much and will do everything to keep you safe and help you discover your own talents and gifts, then yes, you bet there is a God!

Answers to big questions that do not fragment a child's picture of the world, a "cosmic container" for dealing with death, a sense of belonging and of kinship with all creatures, transmittal of core values, a practical understanding of our problematic inner nature, non-magical ways to think about and relate to God—all these and more can be brought to the younger generations by welcoming the epic of evolution into our children's lives. There are two reasons why faith communities must take the lead in this effort. First, extensions of science into realms of meaning and value are so novel and require so much preparatory learning that we cannot expect parents to handle this task on their own. Second, schools will continue to offer few, if any, opportunities for children to learn of their 14-billion-year heritage—and surely no opportunity to explore the personal and practical implications of such knowledge.

My favorite example of these new realizations sums it up well. Michael and I had just arrived for our second turn as theme speakers for a summer camp near Durango, Colorado. A young woman seemed so happy to see me. She said,

> I brought my two boys to your stardust program last time
> you were here. My youngest was only three and a half years
> old then, so I didn't expect him to understand, much less

remember, anything from that experience. But let me tell you what he said just a few weeks ago. I was telling him about something that had happened to our family in the past. He asked, "Mom, was I born yet?" No, I said. "Was I in your belly yet?" No. "Oh," he said, "I must still have been stardust!"

Michael Dowd and I both go about our work of evolutionary evangelism in religious and secular settings guided by this conviction: May the best story win. We don't preach or teach the epic of evolution and its religious implications by saying, "This is the truth, so thou shalt accept it." Rather, we aim to awaken individuals to this perspective primarily because it truly is a great story. The story of our immense collective journey can help us make sense of the world—from our own small dramas outward to the scale of the planet, the galaxy, and beyond. Awakening to this story can inspire and guide each and every one of us toward joyous, on-purpose lives.

Paradise Is Here

Linda Olson Peebles

The life and teachings of Charles Darwin have much to offer us all as we make sense of our selves, our communities, our theologies, and our relationship to the universe. All that learning and growing begins with our direct experience—the observations of the natural world and the meaning we give to that experience. Appreciating Darwin's contributions can inspire in our spirits, especially for those of us who are religious liberals, a sense of wonder in all creation.

Rachel Carson, an environmental scientist, wrote a lovely essay in 1956, later published in an illustrated book called *The Sense of Wonder*. She relates her own discovery of encountering the amazing quality and capacity of a child's learning through the direct experience of nature. She encourages us to realize, "If a child is to keep alive his inborn sense of wonder . . . he needs the companionship of at least one adult who can share it, rediscovering with him the joy, excitement, and mystery of the world we live in."

To keep Darwin and his contributions alive for our children, adults must come to appreciate his life and explore how it relates to their own journeys toward developing meaning and living out a theological stance. Darwin's life offers a chance to reflect on the virtues and challenges of following our deepest calling, the value of exploration, and the impact of offering paradigm-shifting views.

As we grow along on life's journey of learning, it is important for children and adults to see the connection between observing nature and discovering the implications of what we see. Observation can help us develop and articulate our own theology, our sense of beginnings, relationships, meanings, and ethics. Liberal religious theology can discern its creation story through scientific observations and interpretations of biologists, who help us understand the nature of life, and cosmologists, who show us the nature of the universe. Darwin showed that life survives not by strength or power but the ability to keep adapting to changing environments.

Darwin offers us a new chapter for our creation story, to add to the lyrical stories of every people and religion in history. The story the way life evolved has since been refined by others who have looked closely, studied carefully, and discovered new insights from each new bit of evidence. As theologian James Luther Adams once said, "Revelation is not sealed; it is ongoing." Scripture is not sealed; new parts are always being added. The creation story is still being discovered.

We benefit from knowing the old creation stories from around the world, originating with the wisdom of elders and oral tradition. It is good to teach these stories to one another. And we need to know that modern religion has a new creation story, coming from the wisdom of scientists and observed nature. This is the story that we can learn and teach and believe in positively. It is the creation story that fits a theology that honors both the uniqueness and the inter-relatedness of all of creation. It calls us to see diversity as enriching and transformation as life-giving. It helps us to see the paradise already in existence that is ours to savor and to save. This is a universal story, not specific to any one culture or religion or location or time, but shared by all creation as we know it—birthed in the cosmos, and developing on earth.

The new creation story fits well with a liberal religious perspective on the world. The Sources of Unitarian Universalist faith proclaim that truth comes not only from written holy texts. It can be found through direct experience, in words and deeds of prophetic men and women, in humanist teachings that counsel us to heed the guidance of reason and science, and in earth-centered traditions that instruct us to live in harmony with the rhythms of nature. The wisdom of those teachings supports us as we strive to affirm the inherent worth and dignity of each individual, encourage spiritual growth, and respect the interdependent web of all existence. This view of wisdom and of our relationship with creation complements the observations and theories of Darwin.

Darwin and his work offer much to the curious mind. The mind loves to learn from nature and from what can be seen and touched and tasted. Our enthusiasm and insight can make the teachings come alive for adults and children alike.

In order to offer evolution as our creation story—and to make it as lyrical and memorable as any culture's creation story—we need to understand the sense of wonder and power in the unfolding of the natural world. Reverend Forrest Church, of All Souls church in New York City, writes in a sermon,

> Life itself is a miracle. Our very being is predicated against impossible odds, odds infinitely more daunting than winning the lottery. Going back to the very first human beings, all our ancestors lived to puberty, chose the only mate they could have chosen for us to exist, made love at the only possible moment and united the only possible sperm and egg to keep our tenuous prospects alive. Then go back a billion years further, all the way to the ur-paramecium. And back billions of years before that, hedging the earth's bet on the combustion of gasses and the pinball of stars. A single, unbroken thread connects us to the very moment of creation. The Universe was pregnant with us when it was born.

The teachers who have gotten children excited about the big bang, Darwin, evolution, and the scientific process are people who themselves have been caught by the excitement of it all. Their "religious experience" of rapture has as much to do with their direct experience of transcending mystery and wonder, as it does with their intellectual curiosity. Teaching enthusiastically about Darwin's life, especially how his personality and curiosity led him to observe nature, also helps children and adults realize the creativity of the unique human mind. Reflecting on Darwin's inner conflict about presenting a new view of the world offers us not just a history lesson, but an example of the kind of dilemma which we all face in one way or another when we strive to live authentic and compassionate lives.

People who can engage others in exploring the meanings of the life and work of Darwin and others like him can make many connections—within themselves, between various ideas, and with the learners and their experiences. The creation story is the story of our own lives. Discovering it through valuing open minds, hearts, and eyes can inspire us all to explore our home. This isn't to say that teachers and parents won't be challenged by questions and resistance from unexpected places. In his poem "At the Smithville Methodist Church" Stephen Dunn describes a challenging situation that many families could face:

> It was supposed to be Arts & Crafts for a week,
> but when she came home
> with the "Jesus Saves" button, we knew what art
> was up, what ancient craft.
>
> She liked her little friends. She liked the songs
> they sang when they weren't
> twisting and folding paper into dolls.
> What could be so bad?
>
> Jesus had been a good man, and putting faith
> in good men was what
> we had to do to stay this side of cynicism,
> that other sadness.

OK, we said, One week. But when she came home
singing "Jesus loves me,
the Bible tells me so," it was time to talk.
Could we say Jesus

doesn't love you? Could I tell her the Bible
is a great book certain people use
to make you feel bad? We sent her back
without a word.

It had been so long since we believed, so long
since we needed Jesus
as our nemesis and friend, that we thought he was
sufficiently dead,

that our children would think of him like Lincoln
or Thomas Jefferson.
Soon it became clear to us: you can't teach disbelief
to a child,

only wonderful stories, and we hadn't a story
nearly as good.
On parents' night there were the Arts & Crafts
all spread out

like appetizers. Then we took our seats
in the church
and the children sang a song about the Ark,
and Hallelujah

and one in which they had to jump up and down
for Jesus.
I can't remember ever feeling so uncertain
about what's comic, what's serious.

Evolution is magical but devoid of heroes.
You can't say to your child
"Evolution loves you." The story stinks
of extinction and nothing

exciting happens for centuries. I didn't have
a wonderful story for my child
and she was beaming. All the way home in the car
she sang the songs,

occasionally standing up for Jesus.
There was nothing to do
but drive, ride it out, sing along
in silence.

What story do we need to tell our children? Here is my response
to Dunn's poem and to the many parents and religious profession-
als who search for a wonder-filled way to tell our creation story to
children.

When a child wonders where we came from,
We go out into the night and build a fire to keep warm,
        and look up at the sky.
We sing "Twinkle, Twinkle, Little Star"
And sing happily
Because what is inside each of us
Is just like the star.
When a child wonders who loves her, we hold her hands
        and sing
"You Are My Sunshine!"
When families come to share in the potluck, and time
        comes to offer blessing,
We light the Chalice flame, for life and love and memories
        and each other, and sing,
"This little light of mine, I'm gonna let it shine!"

When families bring their pets to be blessed, we sing,
  "We've Got the Whole World in Our Hands!" and
  "All God's Critters Got a Place in the Choir"
Our heroes are
    long-ago people who developed language, fire, art,
      and cooking
    leaders all over the world, like Abraham, Moses, and
      Harriet Tubman,
    who helped people find their way to new places to live
      in peace and freedom
    teachers like Jesus (yes) and the Buddha and others,
    who taught stories about loving people
    and YOU who keep the journey going on!
Our story of evolution
    is NOT of what is extinct.
Our story of evolution IS
    of what survives
    of what has been transformed and lives on
    of what we are becoming
    of the future which lives after us.
Our story is not of disbelief.
Our story is of belief and faith
    in the story of you and you and you,
    in the stories of love and hope,
    in the stories of hurt and reconciliation,
    in the stories of changing and growing.

We people of the one creation, which is still ongoing, have our
old and new stories to tell. And we have the great power of real-
izing that we are part of the new story which is ever evolving, ever
becoming, ever being told. That is the sense of wonder, a gift which
has been handed to us by people like Charles Darwin. Now it is
our turn to pass it on to the next generation, in the paradise we
continue to create here on our earth.

A Saving Message

Fredric Muir

The opportunity for salvation is not something most people think about when ruminating on evolution and natural selection. Yet for many, the lessons—indeed, the truths—that grew from Darwin's work have shaped an essential, vital, and core grounding which has led to a salvific outlook in two ways. First, amidst the destruction of life, with species extinction occurring at an alarming pace, evolutionary theory explains how life developed and is developing. While this is something to marvel at, there is no reason why *Homo sapiens* couldn't be added to the extinction list. Darwin has led us to recognize and name our common roots in this large and complex world; his theory of evolution can help us appreciate the preciousness, fragility, and connectedness of all living things. Because of this, we have the knowledge and motivation to save our species and our planet.

Second, on a more intimate and personal level, evolutionary theory can offer profound meaning to our existence. The neurologist and psychiatrist Oliver Sacks describes this well.

> Evolutionary theory provided, for many of us, a sense of deep meaning and satisfaction that belief in a Divine Plan had never achieved. The world that presented itself to us became a transparent surface, through which one could see the whole history of life. . . . It made life seem all the more precious, and a wonderful, ongoing adventure.

For Sacks, life became inspiring and uplifting because of his relationship to the community of living things. He rejoices in his uniqueness, antiquity, and kinship with all other forms of life.

Any of us may have wondered and pondered these same ideas. This is the product of reflection and awareness, which is where a saving message must always begin. Our attention can raise our awareness of the world around us and of the world inside us. With greater awareness, Sacks's life changed and ours can too. Darwin's life changed—he had the ability to patiently observe detail with intense focus, deliberation, and persistence. In spite of a lack of formal training, he had what it took to be a world-class natural historian and a good scholar. These gifts afforded him both personal pleasure and professional prestige. Some suggest it started at an early age.

An 1816 family painting shows Charles Robert Darwin, age six, kneeling next to his younger sister, Catherine, who is seated. The young Charles is balancing a potted plant on his leg. This painting has been reproduced in print and on film, often paired with a comment such as "Charles's love of nature started at a young age." So it did. His family's social status, wealth, and love for education contributed to a childhood environment that allowed him and his four siblings the freedom and safety to explore the natural world. Surrounded by opportunities for wonder and exploration, they were encouraged to embrace and immerse themselves in nature.

In the painting, Charles is holding the pot with two hands, almost hugging it to keep it balanced. This could be seen as a metaphor for things to come. After leaving the structure of his family and home, Darwin's life became one of seeking balance. At first he balanced his family's expectations—primarily his father's—with his own interests. His father once said, "You care for nothing but shooting, dogs, and rat-catching and you will be a disgrace to yourself and all your family." Despite his father's disappointment (his mother died when he was eight years old), Charles wouldn't walk in his footsteps by becoming a physician. After two years at medical school in Edinburgh, he dropped out. He wanted to pursue his passion for natural history, but his father insisted that he follow a path that would result in a profession worthy of the family name. Robert Darwin believed that the Church of England held the solution: Charles would become an Anglican priest, serving a local parish. If in his free time he wished to study natural history—natural theology—as other clergy did, then so be it. Off to Cambridge Charles went, though decades later, in his autobiography, he questioned his commitment to the church's creeds: "It never struck me how illogical it was to say that I believed in what I could not understand and what is in fact unintelligible. . . . Considering how fiercely I have been attacked by the orthodox it seems ludicrous that I once intended to be a clergyman."

But Darwin was rescued from serving a parish. Rev. John Stevens Henslow, a Cambridge botany professor, recognized in him a unique passion for natural history. When Henslow learned of the need for a natural historian and captain's companion on board the surveying vessel H.M.S. *Beagle,* he recommended Darwin, who was thrilled. Charles enlisted a favorite uncle, Josiah Wedgwood II, to convince Robert Darwin that the proposed two-year circumnavigation would do the boy good. Even after a year at sea, there remained concern regarding what might have happened had Charles stayed home. One of his mentors wrote to Darwin's family, "It was the best thing in the world for him that he went out on the Voyage of Discovery. There was some risk of his turning out an idle man: but his character will now be fixed, and if God spares his life, he will have a great name among the Naturalists of Europe."

The *Beagle*'s two-year voyage stretched from December 27, 1831, to October 2, 1836. While on board, Darwin was seasick most of the time. He read and he wrote letters, in which he often spoke of his homesickness—especially after he realized the voyage would extend beyond two years. Among the several books that he carried and most important to his thinking, as it was for any natural historian of the time, was William Paley's 1802 work, *Natural Theology, or Evidences of the Existence and Attributes of the Deity Collected from the Appearances of Nature.* Paley's thesis, though rejected soon after Darwin returned home, was radical in its own right and had shaped the natural sciences. Before Paley, few were bold enough to suggest that evidence of God could be found outside holy Christian scripture, but Paley argued that this evidence could be found in nature and that it confirmed and conformed to scripture. Darwin's professors had taught him well; when he boarded the ship, he was a disciple of Paley and found no reason to doubt or reject anything Paley said.

In the fall of 1835, the *Beagle* set a course for the Galápagos archipelago, a stop that changed Darwin's life. He saw on the islands reasons to doubt the facts as revealed by Paley. Years after his return, he described in *Voyage of the Beagle* the different beak sizes of finches (which he had misclassified as grosbeaks) on each island—islands that were relatively close together. It didn't make sense: How could members of one species of bird residing in such close proximity have such different distinguishing features? This puzzle haunted him for the next twenty-four years. In less than a year after returning home, he began his journal on evolution by natural selection. For more than two decades he reflected, tested hypotheses, and collected voluminous evidence to support his simple idea that life evolved from adaptation and reproduction aided by long expanses of time.

He also worried. On July 5, 1844, he wrote to his wife, Emma,

> I have just finished my sketch of my species theory. If, as I believe that my theory is true and if it be accepted even by one competent judge, it will be a considerable step in science. I therefore write this, in case of my sudden death, as my most solemn and last request, that you will devote 400£ to its publication.

The letter continues with details of how and when the book was to be published. Why would Darwin's thoughts turn to death at the age of thirty-five? He was often ill, but the letter to Emma was about something greater than physical illness. He was consumed by overwhelming anxiety—dread that he would never have enough evidence to substantiate his claims and anxiety that, when he eventually did publish, the negative reaction from the church, colleagues, friends, and family would isolate and destroy him. We know that Darwin thought of himself as a murderer. Though he was not about to stop his research, he believed he was killing off the Jewish and Christian God. He also felt like a thief. The Talmud distinguishes between a robber and a thief: A robber will hold you up, face to face, and steal your property; a thief will ease into your life and, having won your confidence, slowly strip you of all that you own. Darwin had not confronted Victorian England, as a robber might, and eliminated its convictions, though he believed they were in error. Instead, he had long been one of them, one who could be trusted. If he could have figured out a way to balance the pressures of his work he might have been a happier, more centered man. This kind of equilibrium eluded him.

Despite this, Darwin's work reached far into the depths of science and beyond and gave us new direction, which is amazing if only because he had so little to work with, at least compared to what we have today. He didn't have the ever-lengthening and detailed fossil trail that contemporary scientists enjoy, nor the geological and biological equipment and labs that date artifacts and identify remnants. Although the Austrian monk and scientist Gregor Mendel (1822–1884) was familiar with Darwin's work, the two never communicated. It wasn't until the early twentieth century that scientists understood and appreciated Mendel's discoveries on the mechanism of inheritance, and it was later still before genetic theory and testing became possible. Yet, remarkably, modern breakthroughs and the continuously expanding body of scientific knowledge have not discredited nor replaced Darwin's work—they have only affirmed it. Science journalist Thomas Hayden comments in his article for *Smithsonian* magazine, "What Darwin Didn't Know," "Truly one of the most remarkable traits of Darwinism itself is that it has withstood heavy scientific scrutiny for a century and a half and still manages to accommodate the latest ideas."

Darwin's work created and supported a scientific revolution, but he affected far more than science. Politics, economics, philosophy, and theology were all shaped by his ideas. While he may not have approved of the application of his ideas to fields outside science, there was little he could do about it. His reluctance to bless these ventures is understandable—some were entrepreneurial, misguided, destructive, and self-serving, the kinds of things that Darwin, a gentle and humble man, would have found misleading and presumptuous. He avoided making broad, attention-getting generalizations or pronouncements on the social issues of his day. He rarely attended gatherings where his ideas were presented, argued, or challenged (a group of close friends did this for him). Most of his letters focused on data collection and observation. His scientific conclusions were radical and he maintained strong, progressive political opinions. Yet because of his conservative personal habits and lifestyle, he never made a public display, sharing his strongest feelings only with family and close friends. Still, there is meaningful application of Darwin's work outside the limits of evolutionary biology.

The scientific blueprint left by Darwin became a map for twenty-first century science. His work—what many describe as the single best idea anyone has ever had—is the foundation on which old ideas are verified and new science is validated. Early in his ponderings, Darwin scribbled a blueprint called a "Tree of Life" that served as a metaphor for how he imagined the struggle for existence—"descent with modification through natural selection" (now simply called evolution). Fifteen years before *On the Origin of Species* sold out its first several printings, he understated—as was often his way—just how encompassing his idea was. He wrote in a letter to his wife, "If, as I believe that my theory is true and if it be accepted even by one competent judge, it will be a considerable step in science." And just months before the publication of *Origin,* as he reflected about all those with whom he had shared his ideas and how, one by one, they were coming around to his point of view, he wrote in another letter, "We shall live to see all the *younger* men converts." Darwin knew that his theory was a big deal. He dreaded it being too big a deal, but he was in too deep to stop, he had too much integrity to stop. He knew that this blueprint, his "Tree of Life," was going to have powerful, immediate, and lasting results.

Darwinian evolution stretches past the boundaries of science. His gift to the generations was more than a portrayal of the process that results in life as we know it. His blueprint points us in the direction of salvation. Yes, his is a salvific idea, in the orthodox sense. Darwin's saving message for humankind is about a life on earth not as we have shaped it but as it could be and was intended to be—at least, as intended by evolution. Not for another lifetime but for right now. Darwin's vision can save us from the personal, domestic, and global dread and fear that hold us hostage in our homes and communities. It can liberate us from the root causes and misguided explanations of tribal and nationalistic turmoil. It can save us from the confusion and hostility born of misunderstandings among faith communities. By his work, we can be saved from premature death, from extinction, because the salvation he names is life-giving. It can put us at ease and give us space to welcome and enjoy the heritage and future we share.

This message of salvation contains five lessons or "articles of faith." The first is about change. Of the several truths that define Darwinian evolution, the fact that change never ceases is essential. Change is a law of life; it is an absolute. According to the law of evolution, change can be slow, often measured in thousands of years. It never stops; the earth is in perpetual motion. While Darwin never directly said how the constant of change applies to our lifestyles, it didn't take a lifetime of study to realize just how unsettling his observations could be. If nothing remains the same, then everything around us is unfixed. Like Paley's initial revelations, Darwin's evolutionary faith didn't conform to Church of England theology. The personal God in whom Victorians believed and to whom they sang their songs of praise was unchanging, all powerful, unflinching, shaping every detail. In a favorite hymn by Cecil F. Alexander, parishioners sang with confidence:

All things bright and beautiful,
All creatures great and small,
All things wise and wonderful:
The Lord God made them all.

Each little flower that opens,
Each little bird that sings,
He made their glowing colors,
He made their tiny wings.

The rich man in his castle,
The poor man at his gate,
God made them, high or lowly,
And ordered their estate.

God was in charge and was a deity of stability that had ordained an ordered and rigid structure. Darwin knew he was challenging the status quo by presenting a slow but absolute law of change. He realized he was putting Anglican England's unchanging God and His hierarchy on moving ground.

In most contemporary Anglican hymnals, the third stanza of "All Things Bright and Beautiful," as shown above, is omitted. We can only guess why. Might it be that the church saw the classist, oppressive implications of the stanza and realized that this did not depict the loving, embracing God they wanted to share with all? The God of the original hymn, to whom they sang, was inflexible and limiting—seemingly positioned as a rich man in his castle. Such rigidity shaped an image of God who was unfeeling, whose inflexibility and lack of tenderness could lead Him to crack and crumble. This was a divine power who, despite His marvelous works, was detached from the pain and misery of living things. While Darwin's theory didn't assert that the church's teachings or its frozen God were suspect, many perceived a subtext of skepticism and criticism. These were not church officials, but Darwin's colleagues, many of whom were clergy and believed Darwin had

limited the position of God. Indeed, for Darwin, God's role w
diminishing. Over time, his faith diminished. He wrote in his autobiography, "Disbelief crept over me at a very slow rate, but was at
last complete. The rate was so slow that I felt no distress, and have
never since doubted even for a single second that my conclusion
was correct." His change of heart, theology, and worldview was,
like evolution, a product of time. As an agnostic, he valued and
affirmed his faith in the law of change. And, as poet William Blake
notes, there is comfort and safety—salvation—in change and flexibility. Blake, a contemporary of Darwin, writes:

> Every night and every morn
> Some to misery are born;
> Every morn and every night
> Some are born to sweet delight.

> Joy and woe are woven fine,
> Clothing for the soul divine:
> Under every grief and pine
> Runs a joy with silken twine.

> It is right it should be so:
> We were made for joy and woe;
> And when this we rightly know,
> Safely through the world we go.

The second article of faith we can glean from evolution is the
value and life-giving energy of balance, or in today's parlance, sustainability. Like change, balance is essential to life as we know it,
and Darwin understood this early on. One of the turning points
in his work was the *Beagle*'s stop at the Galápagos; another was
reading the work of Rev. Thomas Robert Malthus. Darwin writes
in his autobiography,

much larger swaths of farmland—are reverting to nature, as people abandon their land and move to the cities in search of better living.

By one estimate, for every acre of rain forest cut down each year, more than 50 acres of new forest are growing in the tropics on land that was once farmed, logged, or ravaged by natural disaster.

Environmentalists would remind us that these new "secondary forests" will never fully replace the ancient and unique rainforest life that has been lost forever. The truth of this devastation must be honored and our losses mourned. Yet the *Times* report confirms that the natural world has its own mechanisms of change and balance that seek sustainability. Evolution's momentum tends to create and sustain life at whatever cost. While we understand these laws of evolution, we must actively promote sustainability for all living things, or the evolutionary process will do it without us. Although we may be "evolution become conscious of itself," as postulated by Jesuit scholar Pierre Teilhard de Chardin, we are not evolution— it's not about us! With or without us, nature, via evolution, is life-seeking. The evolutionary process will always win—"and when this we rightly know, / Safely through the world we go."

The salvific lessons of change and balance contribute to shaping the third article of faith: *Homo sapiens* are not at the center of the world. Although we may be unique, we are not alone. With all species, we compose a finely woven web called life. This was not a new message; in sharing it, Darwin reluctantly joined a short list of those who had revealed that ours is not an anthropocentric world. Nicolaus Copernicus had announced that earth, and therefore humans, are not at the center of the universe. Fortunately for Copernicus, he died in the same year that he published his findings —1543. It was left to his disciples to defend and suffer for what he had started. The Vatican would not stand for this heresy: Giordano Bruno was burned at the stake in 1600 for his extension of the Copernican theory of the heliocentric universe. Galileo Galilei, who documented the facts, died while under house arrest in 1642, though he was welcomed back into the church in 1992. Copernicus, Bruno, and Galileo, along with others, were powerful reminders to Darwin that the support of family, friends, and God could not be taken for granted. They are also strong reminders to us of how absorbed humankind is with itself and the extent to which leadership will go to maintain the status quo. "We are the earth upright and proud; in us the earth is knowing," proclaims a favorite hymn among religious liberals—lyrics that may not place earth at the center of the solar system but nevertheless elevate humankind to a lofty position of knowledge and prominence that for many is unquestionable.

Darwin's depiction of evolution as a Tree of Life, with many stops and starts yet with a common trunk, reflects his understanding that humankind shares a common ancestral past with all living things. Acknowledging this ancient and ongoing shared past should lead us to a profound posture of humility. Thomas Huxley, who called himself "Darwin's bulldog," concluded that the essence of religion "is best expressed in Micah's saying 'What doth the Lord require of thee, but to do justly, and to love mercy, and to walk humbly with thy God?'" Huxley then paraphrased the last phrase: "and to bear himself as humbly as befits his insignificance in the face of the Infinite." Humility, not narcissism, egotism, or anthropocentricism, is the appropriate response to being a twig— not even a branch—on the Tree of Life. In other words, Darwin and his followers did see the process of evolution as a religious insight in the broadest sense. The Latin root of the word *religion* is *religare,* which means "to bind," as in to bind together, as you might do to mend a broken limb. Religion is to be a healing, supportive, nurturing, and unifying experience. Evolution unified all living things; it made sense of life by describing how everything alive is one strand in the web that connects us all.

The twenty-two years that Darwin sat with his ideas had some close calls. The most famous of these came from Alfred Russel Wallace, a field botanist working in Malaysia who, in the summer of 1858, sent Darwin an explanation of natural selection identical to his. So, after two decades of waiting, Darwin published *On the Origin of Species* in a year. Another scoop nearly occurred much earlier, in 1844, with the anonymous publication of *Vestiges of the Natural History of Creation*, a best-seller in England and the United States. There were many who guessed that Darwin was its author. Eventually, a Scottish editor, Robert Chambers, confessed. Darwin was relieved to read that, while there were slight similarities in thought, *Vestiges* was significantly different from his work. Perhaps most revealing is not what Chambers wrote but Darwin's words. On a slip of paper inserted in his copy of *Vestiges*, he wrote: "Never use the word higher or lower." And he wrote to Joseph Hooker, director of the Royal Botanic Gardens, saying, "Heaven defend me from [the] nonsense of a 'tendency to progression.'" Darwin also remarked to him, "An unavoidable wish to compare all animals with men, as supreme, causes some confusion."

Later, Darwin confirmed this idea by writing in one of his notebooks, "It is absurd to talk of one animal being higher than another. *We* consider those, where the cerebral structure/intellectual faculties most developed, as highest. A bee doubtless would when the instincts were." This must have felt like an epiphany, since it was so far out of the mainstream of scientific thinking. It constitutes the fourth article of faith in Darwin's saving message: There is no higher or lower, best or worst—the language of hierarchy, inherent value, or anthropocentric categorizing does not apply to species or to the evolutionary process. The proximity of a species to human beings does not determine its worth. Take away these false divisions of life, and what remains is simply difference. Humans are not higher than dogs, just different; chimps are not more valuable than fish, merely different; finches are not better than worms, but different. With our differences, every living thing within every species is merely trying to "make sense" of life, which is to say, each—including the species *Homo sapiens*—is struggling to maintain life, fighting for existence. Consciously or not, each wants to adapt and survive.

What makes Darwin's deepening realization that humans are not at the top of a hierarchy far more impressive is to understand it through the lens of mid-nineteenth century English culture and his political loyalties. Darwin's family (the Darwins and the Wedgewoods) were fierce abolitionists—their commitment of resources, their outspokenness, and their relationships all directed and gave a depth of meaning to Charles's life, and to his science. In this light, a dramatically different image of Darwin and *Origin* emerges. As Adrian Desmond and James Moore note in *Darwin's Sacred Cause*, Darwin's science became more radical because "slavery, race and evolution remained inseparable." He was embarrassed and angered by how humans behaved and treated other humans. He was boldly condemning not just white, Victorian England but the inhumanity of all. To be sure, Darwin was a product of classist privilege and assumptions. He was subject to the bigotry of his day and held derogatory views that we would call racist today. This makes his conclusions even more profound and revolutionary. It took selfless courage, unflinching vision, and deep certainty to proclaim at the end of *The Descent of Man*, "I would as soon be descended from that heroic little monkey, who braved his dreaded enemy in order to save the life of his keeper; or from that old baboon, who, descending from the mountains, carried away in triumph his young comrade from a crowd of astonished dogs," than take pride in being from those who claim superiority merely because they believe they are of a higher species.

The saving quality of this article of faith rests on the recognition that all living things compose a system, a web, a family. Sharing an ancestral lineage that extends back billions of years, our family system is intricate, unique, and sacred—yet also simple and ordinary, even mundane. While Darwin understood that the individuality of each living thing makes it inherently fascinating and precious, he also uncovered the value of community membership, which is awesome and humbling. If we share a common ancestry, then we share a common future—not just among the human species, but all life— because there is no higher or lower, only the life of all living things.

From his grand voyage on the *Beagle*, Darwin returned to Shrewsbury with a passion for life that would shape his saving message. In his letters home and in *Voyage* and *Origin*, he repeatedly names insights from scenes that thrilled and moved him. Years later, he reconsidered his responses in his autobiography and concluded,

> I well remember my conviction that there is more in man than the mere breadth of his body. But now the grandest scenes would not cause any such convictions and feelings to rise in my mind. It may be truly said that I am like a man who has become colour-blind, and the universal belief by men of redness makes my present loss of perception of not the least value as evidence.

As he approached the end of his years, Darwin may have been exhausted and discouraged. Perhaps the emotional intensity of his labor and the debate had worn him down. Yet the breadth and depth of his accumulated body of work provide a moving and convincing legacy. As Edward O. Wilson writes in *From So Simple a Beginning*,

> The revolution begun by Darwin was even more humbling: it showed that humanity is not the center of creation and not its purpose either. But in freeing our minds from our imagined demigod bondage, even at the price of humility, Darwin turned our attention to the astounding power of the natural creative process and the magnificence of its products.

Darwin gave us a liberating gift: He freed us from the center of the universe, from the grimness of being weighed down by an exaggerated sense of collective self, divorced from the web of life. Now, with a generous spirit, we can see the final lesson of his saving message: Live in wonder, openness, and exploration with the community of life where we make our home. In the end, Darwin knew what was missing from his life; he understood the hardships of the transformation he had initiated and what it could do to one's spirit. He felt the abuse his work inflicted on him. He watched as others took his work and reinterpreted and twisted it to meet their needs. Over time, he lost touch with his complete self, failed to nurture his whole being. As if to caution us, he laments in his autobiography:

> My mind seems to have become a kind of machine for grinding the general laws out of large collections of facts. . . . If I had to live my life again I would have made a rule to read some poetry and listen to some music at least once every week. . . . The loss of these tastes is a loss of happiness, and may possibly be injurious to the intellect, and more probably to the moral character, by enfeebling the emotional part of our nature.

In a controlled and cool style—which is to say, in a Victorian, upper-class manner—Darwin is lamenting more than the missed opportunities of his youth. He is naming the self-inflicted draught he experienced because he neglected the depth and soul of his own revelations. It would take more than music and poetry once a week to bring back the grounding for which he yearned. One hundred fifty years later, since the publication of *Origin*, we have the advantages of time and experience to see clearly what was absent from Darwin's life—immersion in and trust of the ancestral web of existence of which he was a part. He had failed to see and feel his place on the Tree of Life, and to fully mingle his shallow roots with the tree's deep and sturdy roots in order to derive meaning and joy.

Darwin gave us a liberating, transforming, and saving message in these five articles of faith—lessons that urge us to review our posture in the world, to reconsider what we think we know, to reorient ourselves. Let it be our hope, as it was his hope for us, to fully immerse our minds, bodies, and spirits in the soul of the web of life that is our home and our salvation. Let us strive to know and embrace Darwin's inspiring message—a message that could save us and generations to come.

About the Contributors

Connie Barlow, a Unitarian Universalist, is the developer of The Great Story website. Connie's most recent book is *The Ghosts of Evolution.* Her previous books are *Green Space, Green Time: The Way of Science, Evolution Extended: Biological Debates on the Meaning of Life,* and *From Gaia to Selfish Genes: Selected Writings in the Life Sciences.*

Michael Dowd is a United Church of Christ minister and the author of *Earthspirit: A Handbook for Nurturing an Ecological Christianity* and *Thank God for Evolution: How the Marriage of Science and Religion Will Transform Your Life and Our World.* He and his wife, Connie Barlow, travel the country teaching their "Gospel of Evolution" at events sponsored by a diverse group of denominations.

John Gibbons is senior minister of the First Parish Church (Unitarian Universalist) in Bedford, Massachusetts. He is the Unitarian Universalist Association's ambassador to the Transylvanian Unitarian Church, a former president of the Unitarian Universalist Partner Church Council, and chair of the Unitarian Universalist International Funding Panel.

Gary Kowalski is the minister of the First Unitarian Universalist Society of Burlington, Vermont, and the author of several books, including *Revolutionary Spirits: The Enlightened Faith of America's Founding Fathers, Science and the Search for God,* and *The Souls of Animals.*

Naomi King is the minister of the River of Grass Unitarian Universalist Congregation in Plantation, Florida. She was the winner of the Unitarian Universalist Association's 2005 Stewardship Sermon Award.

Fredric Muir is the senior minister of the Unitarian Universalist Church of Annapolis, Maryland, and the author of *A Reason for Hope: Liberation Theology Confronts a Liberal Faith, Heretics' Faith: A Vocabulary for Religious Liberals,* and *Maglipay Universalist: The Unitarian Universalist Church of the Philippines.*

William R. Murry, Unitarian Universalist minister and former president of Meadville Lombard Theological School, is the author of *A Faith for All Seasons: Liberal Religion and the Crises of Life* and *Reason and Reverence: Religious Humanism for the Twenty-first Century.*

Linda Olson Peebles is the minister of religious education at the Unitarian Universalist Church of Arlington, Virginia. She served on the Unitarian Universalist Association Board of Trustees for eight years. She is also an artist and singer/songwriter.

Paul Rasor is director of the Center for the Study of Religious Freedom and professor of interdisciplinary studies at Virginia Wesleyan College. He is a Unitarian Universalist minister and the author of *Faith Without Certainty: Liberal Theology in the 21st Century.*

Minot Judson Savage, 1841-1918, was an American clergyman and writer. After serving for nine years in the ministry of the Congregational Church, he became a Unitarian. He was pastor of the Third Unitarian Church, Chicago; of the Church of the Unity, Boston; and of the Church of the Messiah, New York City.

Resources

Books

Nora Barlow, ed., *The Autobiography of Charles Darwin, 1809-1882,* W.W. Norton and Company, 1958.

> Darwin wrote notes for his autobiography prior to his death. His wife, and later other members of his family, prohibited the full text from publication in the autobiography that was published five years after Darwin's death. Nora Barlow, Darwin's granddaughter, restored—with notes—the original in this volume.

Janet Browne, *Charles Darwin: Voyaging,* Princeton University Press, 1996, and *Charles Darwin: The Power of Place,* Princeton University Press, 2002.

> Browne's two-volume biography is the best, well-written and detailed. The first volume covers Darwin's childhood, education, voyage on the *Beagle,* and early research until 1856.

Andrea Cohen-Kiener, *Claiming Earth as Common Ground: The Ecological Crisis through the Lens of Faith,* Skylight Paths, 2009.

> Gathers insights from ecology coalitions, emerging theologies, and spiritual and environmental activists to rally and inspire people from diverse faith traditions to live up to the challenge of healing our environment. Includes discussion questions.

Charles Darwin, *The Descent of Man, and Selection in Relation to Sex* (1871), Quill Pen Classics, 2008.
Darwin applies his theory of natural selection to human beings and explores the social, racial, and religious consequences.

———, *The Expression of the Emotions in Man and Animals* (1872), Filiquarian, 2007.
Darwin explains how humans and animals display such emotions as fear, anger, disdain, and pleasure.

———, *From So Simple a Beginning: The Four Great Books of Charles Darwin*, ed. Edwin O. Wilson, W.W. Norton and Co., 2006.
With introductions by Wilson, this volume contains Darwin's most-read books: *The Voyage of the Beagle* (1845), *On the Origin of Species* (1859), *The Descent of Man, and Selection in Relation to Sex* (1871), and *The Expression of the Emotions in Man and Animals* (1872).

———, *On the Origin of Species By Means of Natural Selection* (1859), Dover Publications, 2006.
Darwin's views of natural selection, adaptation, the struggle for existence, survival of the fittest, and other concepts that form the foundation of evolutionary theory.

———, *The Voyage of the Beagle: Journal of Researches into the Natural History and Geology of the Countries Visited During the Voyage of H.M.S. Beagle Round the World* (1839), Modern Library Classics, 2001.
Chronicles Darwin's five-year journey around the world on the H.M.S. *Beagle*, during which he began to formulate his theories of evolution and natural selection.

Adrian Desmond and James Moore, *Darwin: The Life of a Tormented Evolutionist,* W.W. Norton and Co., 1991.
> The best single-volume biography of Darwin, a classic.

————, *Darwin's Sacred Cause: How a Hatred of Slavery Shaped Darwin's Views on Human Evolution*, Houghton Mifflin Harcourt, 2009.
> This groundbreaking volume explains many of the cryptic comments found in Darwin's voluminous collection of letters and gives the reader a deeper understanding of his passion for human equality.

Michael Dowd, *Thank God for Evolution: How the Marriage of Science and Religion Will Transform Your Life and Our World*, Plume, 2009.
> Explains why it is now possible to view evolution as a call to deep integrity and how aligning with evolutionary trends can guide those who work to make the world a better place.

Duane Elgin and Deepak Chopra, *The Living Universe: Where Are We? Who Are We? Where Are We Going?* Berrett-Koehler, 2009.
> Brings together cutting-edge science and ancient spiritual wisdom to demonstrate that the universe is a living, sentient system and that we are an integral part of it.

Ursula Goodenough, *The Sacred Depths of Nature,* Oxford University Press, 2000.
> Blends modern science with the quest for spiritual meaning. The author, a cell biologist, looks at topics such as evolution, emotions, sexuality, and death while writing about the workings of nature and living creatures.

Gary Kowalski, *Science and the Search for God,* Lantern Books, 2003.
> Explores fascinating new links between religion and science, with a built-in study guide.

Edward J. Larson, *Summer for the Gods: The Scopes Trial and America's Continuing Debate over Science and Religion,* Basic Books, 1997.
> Larson gives wonderful insights into the "Monkey Trial" and explains the context for the nation's ongoing tension between science and religion.

Jennifer Morgan, *Born with a Bang: The Universe Tells Its Cosmic Story, Book One,* Dawn Publications, 2002.
> The life story of the universe as told to young readers by the universe itself. Comes with color photos, paintings, a timeline, a glossary, and resources.

William E. Phipps, *Darwin's Religious Odyssey,* Trinity Press International, 2002.
> Wonderful research and summary of Darwin's religious struggles and beliefs.

Films

Evolution: Darwin's Dangerous Idea, written and directed by David Espar and Susan K. Lewis, narrated by Liam Neeson, WGBH Boston Video, 2001, 120 mins.
> The first episode of PBS's seven-part presentation on evolution. An excellent and accurate portrayal of Darwin's life following the voyage of the *Beagle*.

Evolution: What About God? written by John Heminway, produced by Bill Jersey, narrated by Liam Neeson, WGBH Boston Video, 2001, 60 mins.
> Explores the tension between science and religion by drawing on real human stories.

"An Hour About the Life and Work of Charles Darwin," *The Charlie Rose Show*, December 14, 2005, 60 mins.
> Conversation with scientists E.O. Wilson and James Watson.

Kansas vs. Darwin: Whose Side Are You On? directed by Jeff Tamblyn, produced by Jeff Tamblyn and Jeff Peak, written by Jeff Tamblyn and Mark Con Schlemmer, Unconditional Films, 2007, 82 mins.
> Award-winning documentary about the Kansas evolution hearings in May 2005. The Kansas state school board again captures the world's attention with its evolution controversy—this time by holding scientific hearings that put Darwin's long-held theory on trial.

Paradise Lost: The Religious Life of Charles Darwin, written and directed by David Wollert, narrated by Garry Smith, Black Slate Studios, 2007, 49 mins.
> Incorporating voice-overs from his journals and autobiography, the film traces Darwin's personal and professional life as it documents his transition from theism to deism to agnosticism.

WEBSITES

"A Celebration of Darwin, Science and Humanity," Darwin Day Celebration
> www.darwinday.org

"The Complete Works of Charles Darwin Online"
    www.darwin-online.org.uk

"Darwin Resources for Community Life," Unitarian Universalist
Church of Annapolis, Maryland
    www.uuca-md.org/darwinresources

"The Evolutionary Times," Michael Dowd
    www.evolutionarytimes.org

"The Great Story: An *Epic of Evolution* Educational Website,"
Connie Barlow
    www.thegreatstory.org